Wolfen Wicca 2; Our Walk Onward To Initiation

Wolfen Wicca 2; Our Walk Onward To Initiation

Lady Wolfen Mists

Wolfen Wicca Level 2
Our Walk Onward To Initiation

Lady Wolfen Mists

Copyright © 2015 Lady Wolfen Mists

All rights reserved.ISBN:

978-0-9790662-5-2

Pictures Licensed/Bought from www.123rf.com from various photographers

DEDICATION

This book is Dedicated to those who walk this long often lonely path, trying t find where they "fit." This is to welcome you to your Pack and show you the Magick inside you. You are a part of the Divine spark, my job is to nurture you and guide you how to better access your most positive Higher Self all the while keeping true to that "wild wolf" inside us all.

To; My Students

From: Lady Wolfen Mists

Greetings Student,

Welcome to the new class, I hope you enjoy it as much as I enjoyed putting it together for you. You will notice that throughout the course there may be typos, bad grammar and mis spellings, this isn't because it wasn't checked. It is because it slipped through the editing process and to be frank it's the way I talk. ☺ Yep reading these class are almost like talking directly to me, I was going to change them and make them more professional, more correct with grammar and all, but when I told some of my other students they said don't! That reading the classes was almost like sitting across from me at a table and gave a much cozier feeling than perfection on sterile paper. That my writing (way of talking) to the students was part of the charm of the class and made everyone feel better about themselves. So I kept it the way it is.

I am probably one of the most down to earth people you will ever meet and I don't get really anal (or hung up) about spelling, grammar or typos. I just do my best and expect to make a few writing mistakes, so please forgive any that may appear in advance. The information given in this class is solid and valid and comes from my experiences. Perfect or not in its presentation, it is a work (with sweat, crying, hair pulling and pride) given in love to each of my students. It is my hope that it will help you on your Spiritual Journey. That it is something 20 years from now, you will recall with warmth and love in your heart.

Now with all that said, lets get to the good stuff and open your first class.

Blessings,

Lady Wolfen Mists

ACKNOWLEDGMENTS

I wish to take this time to mention so many of "my pack" who crossed over. To Lady Spirit Dancer, who loved life and so many people. To Lord Dragon Rider, who always had a song for us and was my rock to lean on. To Lord Crystal Wanderer. who was always there for me....there will NEVER be a Fetch to replace you. To Hart Soul Eagle Spirit, who was a ray of Light to us all. To Laugh Dragon, there are no words to describe you and the Light you shared...I miss you so. To all those Lords and Ladies and all those Dedicants, who have crossed over and inspired me in your daily walk, I thank you for being a part of my life. I will never forget you, You will always have a place in my eternal heart.

I Also wish to mention those who made Silver Hoofs (my Store) and my developing Wolfen Wicca possible. They were there at the beginning as I opened on April 1st 1990 and stood by me as I fought to learn to use the computer and wrote these lessons. Lady Shadow Stalker, Lady Quill Master, Lord Forest Walker (whose names have changed as they developed over the years but to me they will always be those named here) a huge THANK YOU. Through the years we have had our ups and downs but truer friends I could have never dreamed of. I love you all seems small to express my feelings for you, yet it is all I have.

Sabbats of Northern & Southern Hemispheres

This is a chart of the Sabbats on both hemispheres, North and South. Although this book is written from the Northern perspective, because that's where I live. you can easily adjust it to the Southern Hemisphere. As such I added this chart so every one is included in the Wolfen Wicca Tradition. Make it your Magick where ever you are.

Sabbat	Northern Hemisphere Approx.	Southern Hemisphere Approx.	Colors
Samhain The Lord dies and awaits his rebirth at Yule	Oct. 31	April 30/ May 1	Orange & Brown
Yule The Goddess gives birth to the God	Dec. 21	June 20-23	Purple or Dark Green Or Red
Imbolc The God is a young child growing in size and strength	Feb. 2	July 31/ Aug 1	Pink or Pale Green
Ostara The God and Goddess begin their courtship	March 21	Sept 20-23	Light Green
Beltain The Lord and Lady consummate their relationship	May 1	Oct 31	White, Red & Pink
Litha The Goddess is pregnant with the God	June 21	Dec 20-23	White & Pale Yellow
Lughnasadh A Festival of life/abundance, of harvest/death	Aug. 1	Feb 2	Gold & Bright Yellow
Mabon The God now sleeps within the womb of the Goddess	Sept. 21	March 20-23	Dark Brown & Red

Wolfen Wicca 2; Our Walk Onward To Initiation

Lady Wolfen Mists

CONTENTS

Class #1	**Theory**	6
	Magickal Wood Information	7
	Magickal Wood: Oil Recipe	11
	Moon Water Oil Recipe	14
	Sabbat Candles	16
	Color Zodiac Color List & Astral Color List	18
	Candle Types	20
	Practical	
	Spell Casting:	
	"Clean Up your act/Environment"	24
Class #2	**Theory**	30
	Components of a spell	31
	Basic Herbal & Herbal List	34
	Herbal Bath Recipe	39
	Magickal Herbal List	42
	Jar Magick: General Info.	44
	Metaphysical Correct Holy Water Recipe	45
	Practical: Make a Witches Wish Jar	46
Class #3	**Theory**	50
	Touching the Source of the Father	51
	Triple aspects of the God	53
	Hex Signs	54
	Traditional Color meanings Hex Signs	57
	List of God Names & Attributes	58
	Practical:	
	Ritual Healing For the Earth	64
Class #4	**Theory**	70
	Reincarnation	71
	Karma general overview	74
	Karma Wolfen Wicca View	77
	Perfect Love & Trust: What it means	82
	Honor	84
	Uncross and Send Back	88
	Past Life Guided Experience	

Wolfen Wicca 2; Our Walk Onward To Initiation

Class #5	**Theory**	96
	Glossary of Common terms	97
	List of Goddess Names	106
	Intro Wards	110
	Wards, How to make them	112
	Your Sacred Sanctuary	117
	Practical:	
	Making a Ward	123
Class #6	**Theory**	126
	Types of wolves in the magickal sense	127
	Familiars in General	132
	Familiar Spell	134
	Familiar Oil Recipe	138
	Color Chart to refer to	139
	Magickal Sand Painting	142
	Symbols	144
	Practical:	
	Magickal Sand Mosaic	147
Class #7	**Theory**	150
	Inside the circle: Reversal Polarity	151
	Magickal Tool: The Besom	153
	Steps to a simple Besom Chart	158
	Wolf Protection Potpourri Recipe	160
	Working with the stone: Onyx	162
	Practical:	
	Protecting your home with onyx	165
Class #8	**Theory**	170
	Explain the Ten (10) planes	171
	Explain the Tree of Life	176
	Weather Magick	178
	Wind Chart	180
	Air Oil Recipe	181
	Weather Working Dust recipe	182
	Weather Magick- Omens	184
	Practical:	
	Storm Magick Spell: Whistle Up the Wind	186

Class #9	**Theory**	190
	Amulets & Talismans & General	191
	Faery Trivia	196
	The Four (4) Elements	198
	The Four (4) Elements Chart	200
	Magickal Wells	202
	Samhain: Overview of Traditions	204
	Samhain Sabbat Group & Solitary	207
	Practical:	
	Do Circle casting & Invoke Talisen	215
*Class #10	**Theory**	218
	Auras --The Three (3) levels	219
	Auras --How to See them	222
	Color & Color Treatment	224
	Music & its effect on Auras	226
	Colors and use	227
	Aura Recording body chart	228
	Tracker Wolf Oil Recipe	229
	Tracker Wolf Pathwork	230
	Practical:	
	Using your Tracker Wolf Pathwork	232
Class #11	**Theory**	234
	Drawing Down the Moon	235
	Positions Drawing Down the Moon	237
	Drawing Down The Moon Rite/Ritual	239
	Charge	242
	Sabbat Info.	245
	Where to place the altar	248
	Triple Goddess potpourri recipe	250
	Myth of the Goddess	251
	Practical:	
	Circle Cast Mock walk through on Drawing Down the Moon	253
Class #12	**Theory**	256
	Long Rede	257

Wolfen Wicca 2; Our Walk Onward To Initiation

Its all in the Perspective	260
DARKNESS vs Dark/shadow self	263
5 fold Kiss	265
Traditions	268
Pagans You should know	272
Coven Offices	274

Practical:

Amulet for Good Luck	277

Class #13 Theory — 280

Degree Symbols	281
Poppet Use	283
Poppet Pattern	285
Poppet Protection	286
Poppet get Money	288
Asking Directions	290
What is a Triskele (Trisklion)	292
Facial Analysis	295

Practical:

Create a poppet	297

Class #14 Theory: — 300

Mirrors of Protection	301
Potpourri: Crossing of a loved one	303
Invoke Goddess	304
Invoke God	305
Thou Art Goddess	306
Create a Fairy Tree	308
Initiation ritual Group & Solitary	310

Practical:

Do Initiation Ritual	314

Lady Wolfen Mists

Wolfen Wicca 2
Our Walk Onward To Initiation
Class #1

© Lady Wolfen Mists Jan.1990

revised 2001

Theory:

    Magickal Wood Information

    Magickal Wood: Oil Recipe

    Moon Water Oil Recipe

    Sabbat Candles Color

    Zodiac Color List & Astral Color List

    Candle Types

Practical:

    Spell Casting: "Clean Up your act/Environment"

"I Walk On"

Wolfen Wicca 2
Class #1
Magickal Wood; Where the Spirits Dwell

© Lady Wolfen Mists

It is a dark night and the moon slowly rises overhead. The cool crispness of the night washes over you, your skin chills. You reach up to the clasp at your throat, pulling at it, drawing your cape closer around you. Feeling secure and safe in the warmth of the enveloping cloth, you can hear your own heart beating. You adjust the hood, pulling it down across your face, fading into the security of the shadows you cast. Continuing to make your way through the woods, you see huge bonfires aglow, in the distance. The flames coloring the darkness in vivid oranges, reds and yellows. The colors leaping and dancing in the natural rhythms of the burning wood and the wind. You hear voices in the distance, laughing and singing, a celebration is going on. A smile crosses your face, knowing this is your destination for the evening, the Sabbat Needfire/Bonfire! This sacred bonfire burns to honor the Lady and Lord, it contains the nine (9) sacred woods, burning within the circle.

Hearing a noise to your right, you look. There within a tall grove of trees sits a large White Owl. Huge brown/black eyes reflect what little light the moon casts this night. Eyes seemingly set in mid-air, peering down at you from yet another sacred gathering place. The wind ruffles through the leafs. The owl stretches out its 6 foot

Wolfen Wicca 2
Class #1-Magickal Wood; Where the Spirits Dwell (p.2)

© Lady Wolfen Mists

wings, as if testing the wind. The air within the grove seems to suddenly be charged with many magickal energies this night. Lifting itself up on its ghostly glowing wings, the owl flies towards the bonfire. Gliding on the magickal currents, as if to go ahead and announce your coming. You quicken your pace, those same energies drawing you to the burning Needfire ahead.

Wouldn't it be wonderful to actually be a part of the Sabbat described above! But to fully appreciate what is happening, one needs to understand the importance of the symbolism of the trees/wood, to the practitioners of the Old Ways.

Trees were/are revered as highly magickal and sacred by followers of the Old Religion, with a special emphasis on the Druids. Woods were commonly used in the construction of divination tools, as well as the entire living tree being used in the making of future predictions. Forest tree folk like Sprites, Spirits, Faries and Devas and Dryads (just to name a few) were said to use the special trees they lived in to communicate with Humans. They would speak by sending their whispers on the wind. The wind in turn would blow through the branches of the tree, delivering their messages in the rustling of the leafs. Often gifts like Creativity, Inspiration, 2nd Sight, and Healing knowledge were conferred on select individuals in this manner, from the tree Spirits.

To the Ancient Celts trees and woods were so important in their culture that they based an early alphabet/language (Called Oghams) on the different types of sacred trees. Today trees and wood are still venerated by pagans, and used in the construction of Magickal Tools. Tools like Pentacles, Athame Handles, Statues, Salt & Water Bowls, Chalices, Talismans, Altars, and many other Magical/ritual items. Oh, and of course wood is often used in the construction of Magickal Wands, also called An-Shet and Fire-Sticks.

Other uses for wood include, but are not limited to, the construction of Sabbat Bonfires/Needfires. These fires

Wolfen Wicca 2
Class #1-Magickal Wood; Where the Spirits Dwell (p.3)

are traditionally made out of Nine (9) Sacred Woods. These woods include:

Ash	Hawthorn
Birch	Holly
Cherry	Oak
Fir	Pine
Rowan	

(Apple and a few others can be substituted as needed in the construction of these fires, if the above listed woods are unavailable)

Special fires, like those for Handfastings or Crossings, can also be built for any occasion. However special regard should b made to those aspects of the Lady and Lord you wish to invoke. Also the Symbolism of the wood to be used, the needed/wanted outcome, the preferences of the participants involved, the odor that the burning wood will create/release, and the availability of the specified woods in your area, all need to be considered when planning the construction of a Bonfire/Needfire. But what ever occasion or type of Bonfire/Needfire you decide to create, the building and burning of it always be a, deeply moving and spiritual act for you. One that you are sure to remember for many years to come, for there is nothing more ancient or wild then the bonfires that speckled the hillsides, as our ancestors once did.

Where The Spirits Dwell!

Wolfen Wicca 2
Class #1
Magickal Wood Oil Recipe

© Lady Wolfen Mists

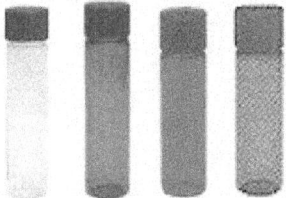

Here is a simple oil used in the Construction and Consecration of Magick wooden tools. Give it a try, I think you will like it. To keep your oil fresh, be sure to store it in a dark colored (amber) glass bottle, in a cool place. Oils last anywhere from 6 months to a year depending on how well they are stored; the less light that gets to the oil the longer the oil will last.

Items Needed:

3 oz. of Grapeseed Oil

2-4 drops of Glycerin

3 drops Rosemary Oil

8 drops of Thyme Oil

13 drops of Verbena Oil

8 drops Sandalwood Oil

Mix these items slowly. Allow oil to sit in Moon light for at least 24 continuous hours. Then funnel it into your vial and be sure to label and date the vial so you don't forget what it is and when you made it. Next place some on a lint free cloth and rub on the wood. It should shine and glisten when oil is applied. You should be able to feel the energy level of your item rise as you add your oil. **After oil**

dries on wood fully, store wooden item in the color red (silk is best but any thing red will work, until used or until given away.) Remember that oil does stain so keep that in mind when storing items in cloth.

Notes from your Brewing

Lady Wolfen Mists

Wolfen Wicca 2
Class #1
Moon Water Oil Recipe

© Lady Wolfen Mists

This is a very old and successful oil that is used to add positive energies, with focus, intent and concentrated will to items, especially in Candles and Candle work. I like it for general dressing of candles in spellwork, that have specific needs for the candles used. This oil helps to harness the energies of the moon itself, to pin point perfection. It's something I love to have on hand and very useful.

Storage:

To keep your oil fresh, be sure to store it in a dark colored (amber) glass bottle, in a cool place. Oils last anywhere from 6 months to a year depending on how well they are stored; the less light that gets to the oil the longer the oil will last.

Items Needed:

1/4 cup of Grapeseed Oil

12 drops of Sandalwood

12 drops Lemon

12 drops of Ylang Ylang

6 drops of Musk

Mix these items slowly. Allow oil to sit in Moon light for at least 24 continuous hours. Then funnel it into your vial and be sure to label and date the vial so you don't forget what it is and when you made it.

To use:

Next place some on a your fingertip or a q tip and anoint the items you select to use or Dress your candle as you were taught to do in the Wolfen Wicca A Beginners Journey Book. You should be able to feel the energy level of your item rise as you add your oil. Remember that oil does stain so keep that in mind when using.

Wolfen Wicca 2:
Class #1:
Sabbat Colors for Candles

    Many times when getting ready to celebrate a sabbat or in constructing a spell I need to know what the colors of a specific sabbat are. This Table gives you the sabbat and the traditional colors used in representing or corresponding to that sabbat.

    Many Practitioners not only decorate their altars with the appropriate color candles; they also have robes made for each sabbat. These robes sport specific colors for that specific sabbat, some even have sabbat symbols incorporated in their design.

Sabbat	Corresponding Color
YULE (Winter Solstice)	Red & Green
IMBOLC (Candlemas)	White or Green & White or Blue
OSTARA (Spring Equinox)	White, Pastels
BELTANE (May Day)	White, Vivid Colors (ie Apple Green)
MIDSUMMER (Summer Solstice)	White, Rich Deep Colors(i.e. Forest Green)
LAMMAS (Lughnadadh)	Red & Orange
MAYBON (Fall Equinox)	Red & Brown
SAMHAIN (Hallowmas)	Red or Black or Pumpkin Orange

And the Great Wheel Turns,

8 Sabbats Burn

As the Seasons Pass By

Goddess & God Live and Die

Quote (chant) by Lady Wolfen Mists

Lady Wolfen Mists

Wolfen Wicca 2
Class #1
Zodiac Candles = Astral Colors Table

Zodiac sign	Corresponding Astral Color
Aries	Red
Taurus	Red Orange
Gemini	Orange
Cancer	Yellow Orange
Leo	Yellow
Virgo	Yellow Green

Libra	Green
Scorpio	Blue Green
Sagittarius	Blue
Capricorn	Blue Violet
Aquarius	Violet
Pisces	Red Violet

When in doubt of what astral color to use, use white as it is the all inclusive of all colors!

Wolfen Wicca 2
Class #1
Common Types of Candles & Uses

© Lady Wolfen Mists

Below is a list of commonly found candles, most can be found at any Metaphysical store. This list tells you what the candles are typically used for, as well as the typical colors. However remember this is just meant a guide, nothing is written in stone, so don't let it hold your inventiveness back.

Types of Candles	**Description**
Tapers	Long, thin, grows narrow at the top Typical "Dinner" Candles
Votive	Short, squat candles, burn in special glass Votive holder
Jumbos	Approx. 9 inches long & 3/4 inch diameter Excellent for spells, easy to carve symbols on
Beeswax	Made with Honeycomb, more expensive than tapers. Burn cleaner & longer

Double Action or Reversible	Like Jumbo but they have one color at one end and another at the other. Use to combine 2 influences or more into one candle. usual colors are Black &White, Red& White, Green& White
Triple Action	Like Double Action, but combines 3 influences or more. Usual colors include: Red, White & Blue or Red, White & Green or Black, Red, White
Astral/Zodiac	These are candles like any of the above, in a color which represents the zodiac sign of the person involved in the spell
Seven Knob or Wish Candle	A Tall candle with 7 balls or knobs. Usually the segments are burnt individually in a 7 day spell, i.e. A Money Drawing Spell. Typical colors: Green, White, Red, Black
Image	Female or Male shaped candles, used to represent the person the spell is being cast for. Typical colors: Red, White, Black
Cat	Cat shaped candle, used to represent a familiar or to empower a spell with "Hidden Knowledge" Usual colors:

	Black, Green, Red
Skull	Candle in the shape of Human Skull, used to break the power of someone who has been cursed or jinxed. Also used in the separation of a person from a job or another person. Typical colors: Black, White
Unicorn	Candle in the shape of a unicorn, used to represent Purity, Healing and eternal Love. Colors vary
Goddess	Candle in the shape of the form of the Goddess. Used to represent female energies or to add extra empowerment to a spell. Also used in female "Rites of passage" rituals. Colors vary but Purple is popular

"Be Like a Candle In the Darkness and SHINE!"

Wolfen Wicca 2:
Our Walk Onward to Initiation
Class #1
Practical: To Clean up Your Act/Environment

©Lady Wolfen Mists

Below is the general overall outline used for the practical section of this class. I've included this so if you have a specific question you can go directly to that section and find the answer quickly. I hope you find it helpful.

1. Purpose:

2. Items Included:

3. Special Information:

4. Steps to Preparation:

5. Special Storage Needs:

6. Clean Up:

7. Recharge Procedure

Additional Items Needed: Moon Water Oil from Class 1

1)   The purpose of this spell is to aid you in getting your house in order and purifying yourself. Everyone steps off the Lighted path now and then. It's often not meant to have happened, but it does. When it

Wolfen Wicca 2
Class #1-
Practical (homework); To Clean up Your Act (pg.2)

does happen one often has trouble cleaning away the garbage and negative energies, and getting back on the positive track. That's what this spell does! Casting this spell once or twice should be enough to clear up the energies around you and take care of the problem.

2.) **Items Included**   **Additional Items Needed**

Items Included	Additional Items Needed
1-White Taper	Moon Water Oil to dress candle
1-Green Taper	
1-Yellow Taper	
1-Red Taper	
1-Blue Taper	

3.) This spell seems most successful during a waxing or full moon. However, if there is a strong need to use it before those moon phases, go ahead and give it a try.

4) (A). Dress the candles in Moon Water Oil and visualize the white candle becoming you. Next dress the taper and "see" them becoming your shields and protectors. "Believe" that nothing negative can get by them. "See" them dissolve negative energies, and replace them with twice as much positive energies.

(B). Set the white candle in the center of the altar when you are finished putting your energies into it. Put the Green candle in the north position above you. The Yellow candle goes to the East, Red to

Lady Wolfen Mists

Wolfen Wicca 2
Class #1-
Practical (homework); To Clean up Your Act (pg.3)

the South and Blue to the West. Do this so the (4) four tapers encircle the white candle.

(C). Light the image candle and say:

"This candle is to represent me. This clean fire burns the negative energies out of me. Cleansing and purifying my mind, body and soul. The fall I took has taken its toll."

(D). Light the tapers and say the following, once for each color. Start with the GREEN candle and work in a deosil manner. Say the following:

"This (color) candle I do Light, Invoking the Watchers and all their might. Cleanse me, protect me and keep me from harm. That I may walk with the Light forever, arm and arm.

(E). Once you have invoked all the Watchers, visualize them, cleaning you, touching you. Leading you to the balance of the soul and the cosmos. Meditate on this balance. Let the candles burn for about fifteen (15) --twenty (20) minutes. "Believe and Know" that your spell has been cast and it's a success!!!!!!

5) No special storage needs

Wolfen Wicca 2
Class #1-
Practical (homework); To Clean up Your Act (pg.4)

6) Clean up as normal

7) There is no recharging of this spell, it must be completely recast if you wish to do it again.

Notes from Class One

Lady Wolfen Mists

Wolfen Wicca 2
Our Walk Onward To Initiation
Class #2

© Lady Wolfen Mists Jan.1990 revised 2001

Theory:

    Components of a spell

    Basic Herbal & Herbal List

    Herbal Bath Recipe

    Magickal Herbal List

    Jar Magick: General Info.

    Metaphysical Correct Holy Water Recipe

Practical: Make a Witches Wish Jar

Circle Work: What is your inspirational thought for the week.

Students in your Magickal Journal: Explain, in writing, why you chose the particular items that you did for the spell. What is the importance of including all the components of a spell into your spell work. (for example what would happen if you left out a step?). This will be reviewed when you submit your work for Initiation ☺

"I WALK ON!"

Wolfen Wicca 201
Class #2
Components of a Spell

Successful spellcasting is often hard for many new Craft members to achieve. try as they might they often report that their spells just don't seem to work or they just don't get the desired results. Well there's no real magical secret to spell casting, but there is a basic methodology that should be followed. A spell is a **very strong visualization technique**, visualization is the key. You must "see" what you want to happen happening **without any doubt.** Doubt will chip away at your focus intent and leaves an opening for a different or no out come at all. Depending on the level of doubt you show is equal to the outcome you receive from the universe. So NO DOUBT! That sounds easy doesn't it? What's that you say, you tried that and it still didn't work. Well... ok ....maybe there are a few extra steps I left out.

There are 5 main steps, that need to be included to insure your success, along with tremendous amounts of visualization. They are :

1.Reason for the spell: Have it clearly in your head why you are casting the spell. Not just "I want to get a job." More like "I need to get a job so that I can take care of my bills and live." get the picture? Clear, concise and to the point.

2. What you want the end result to be: Know exactly what it is you are asking the Universe to manifest for you. Have in mind a clear picture and a time frame. Don't be to restrictive on the time frame, allow the universe a reasonable time (say 30 days) to put into action what you request. Tell The Universe you will accept nothing less than what is best for your Higher Self.

3. Know before you are ready to cast your spell the Type of magick you are going to be using. Remember the 101 class on Sympathetic vs. Contagious magick. Know what type "feels" more comfortable for you and use that one. Maybe you will use a combination of the many types available but know before you cast exactly what your going to do and what your going to say.

Class #2
Components of a Spell Page 2

    4. <u>Material (items) to be used in the spell:</u> Have a written list of items that you will be using in your spell. Many practitioners write their spells much like a recipe, with the title and moon phase at the top, items listed under that, special instructions under that. Then the spell its self. With a written list you can check off ahead of time the items you will be using. There is nothing worse then going along in a spell, feeling the power rising and the energy building. Your at a point where you light a purple candle, you reach for the candle...it isn't there. Now you remember its on the desk downstairs! Now you must cut open the circle to leave, releasing some of the energy built already, go get the candle and re-enter your circle. Much of the power has dissipated by this time and your focus is shot! Timing is critical in spell casting, there's a point when you feel the power and you release it! Don't worry you'll know when you feel it. But what to do with this spell now? I suggest to clean up and start over, its very hard to re-create the type of energy needed when the spell has been disturbed in the process of casting. Some practitioners differ in this opinion with me and say just pick up where you left off. I feel you should just wipe the slate clean and start over! An even better thing to do is check your list beforehand to make sure this doesn't happen at all!

    5. <u>Words of Power:</u> This is the final component that needs to be added for successful spellcasting. You must include in your spell specific Words of Power that you will use as a key (signal) to send your will (the spell) out into the Universe. These words act as the climax for all the power, feeling, intent and want you have set up in your sacred place. These words when spoken releases the energy (spell) into the universe. When spoken these words begin the manifestation of your spell. Now they can be very dramatic (IE."As in the days of the Ancients I set forth these energies to do my will, that all may be as I have written it to be") or very simple (IE."So mote it be"). But they must signal to yourself, and anyone else casting the spell, that this draws together completely, all that we have conjured here. That the words act as the focus point of those energies, and when spoken, releases forth the energies, to do as we wish. Words of Power, although fairly simple, are almost as important as the visualization used upon the release of the energies. They are the power behind the ideas and the intent and <u>must be present</u> to succeed.

    So there you have it, the components of successful spellcasting. Each one is necessary and builds on the next, maintaining that ever present thought/act in Wicca BALANCE. A balance of thought energy and intent must be struck, without even one of these steps you make for a very weak foundation, risking an incomplete spell with less than satisfactorily results.

    On Last note on Spellcasting is a reminder that NO is an answer too! If you send out a spell, lets say 3 times and are not getting the results you are asking for that may be the Universe saying NO to you, as it has something else being made ready for you that will be in your Highest good and what you are requesting will only set

Class #2
Components of a Spell Page 3

obstacles in place that is not in your Highest betterment. Consider this deeply and tell the universe you yield to its knowledge and ask only for what ever is in your Highest good to be send as soon as possible.

Wolfen Wicca 2
Class #2
Basic Herbs and their Traditional uses

Before beginning this section I must, for legal reasons, state that none of this is meant in anyway to replace a Physicians care. Herbal uses are to be used in addition to prescribed medical care and with the full knowledge of your regular physician. I do not wish to misrepresent myself or my skills, as I do not have any formal medical training, that would be accepted by the AMA or the law concerning this issue. Furthermore I am not trying to diagnose or prescribe any type of medical care. I am merely giving you a list of herbs and their traditional uses. If you decide to use any of these herbs, please do so with the full knowledge and approval of your regular physician. I am in no way responsible for any experimentation you may do with these herbs or with your decision to use or not use them in the traditional manners described. Now with all the legalities met, lets move on.

The following is a list of thirteen (13) herbs that are useful in the holistic cabinet of health. They give you a good basis to build from and if you are truly interested in herbal remedies this is a wonderful place to start. Most are easily available at stores most are inexpensive, and easy to use. So here we go:

Name & CAUTIONS	Medicinal part:	Flowering time:	Information on use
Catnip:	The herb	June-Sept.	This herb used in tea form is said to aid upset stomach, colic, flatulence, acid. It is also used as a sleep inducer and to suppress High Fevers

			without suppressing healing in any way
Camomile:	Flowers	June & July	Said to act as a light natural sedative. Can be used as an external wash or poultice for toothaches, earaches, any type of inflammations (i.e. boils) The flowers can be made into a oil for rubbing on sore or swollen joints.
Coltsfoot:	Leaves & Flowers	Summer	Said to be used successfully in most respiratory problems colds, coughs, bronchitis, bronchial asthma, pleurisy, diarrhea. Can be applied as a poultice over lungs & throat. Externally for insect bites, general swelling, burns, phlebitis
Plantain: Common name:Mint	Leaves	July-Sept	Traditionally used as a blood detoxifier for such things as poison Ivy, Bee stings, bug bites. To bites apply crushed fresh leaves. If the cases are severe, drink the tea, eat leaves and re-apply the poultice. Can also be used for bladder problems & gastrointestinal ulcers. Chewing the root is said to give temporary relief from tooth aches.

Lady Wolfen Mists

Cayenne: **Caution:** Excessive internal use can cause kidney damage & gastroenteritis. Prolonged application to the skin may cause dermatitis to the skin and/or raise blisters.	Fruit	April-Sept	This herb does not burn the area it comes into contact with, although it may feel that way. It is used to stop bleeding inside and out, just sprinkle on open cuts. Also said to normalize blood pressure, aids in heart disease, strokes, stomach ulcers.
Comfrey:	Rootstock Flowering	May-Aug.	Called the "Heal All" heals all tissues in the body. Roots and leaves used for broken bones,(i.e. fingers) in trauma. Ointment used in sunburns. Makes an excellent gargle & mouth wash for bleeding gums & throat inflammation burns, loss of any tissues
Echanatia: Common name: Purple cone flower	Rootstock	June -Oct.	This plant is traditionally used as an antiseptic, digestive aid, blood purifier, sinus conditions. Aids conditions like eczema, acne, boils, when used in tea form. Used externally in combination with myrrh it is good to reduce the effects of typhoid fever
Garlic:	The bulb	time: Varies	It is important to skin,

Caution: Garlic oil **will** burn skin. Do not apply full strength or fresh cut directly on the skin	Flowering		hair, digestion, lungs, blood. Traditionally used as a natural antibiotic, for earaches steep in olive oil and drop into ear, warm. Lowers blood fat & pressure.
Ginger:	Rootstock Flowering	Summer	Used to relax. In tea form used to relax after over eating, handy during the holidays. Also said to end cramps, and induce perspiration in colds & fevers. Used to tone bowl muscles, great for after pregnancy, or truck drivers
Goldenseal: Common name: Tumeric Root **CAUTION:** Eating Fresh plant can produce inflammation of mucous tissue, as well as ulcerations. Use dried plant only Goldenseal continued	Rootstock	Summer	Traditional uses include antiseptic, astringent, laxative, general tonic, stomach ailments, colds & flu. Overall Healer. Popularly used as internal (tea, as described above) & external (wash, open sore, rashes, eczema) uses. Small doses taken during pregnancy will help relieve nausea.
Lobelia: Common Name: Indian Tobacco, Wild Tobacco **CAUTION BELOW**	the plant	July-Nov	Used as a anti-spasmodic, used to calm physical (epilepsy) or emotional tissue. Used as a pain reliever.

Caution: There should be some caution when using. **Some reports state that it is Poisonous,** there is said to be a real potential for harm if used incorrectly.			
Peppermint: Common name: Mint	Leaves	July-Sept.	Used in tea form for Migraine, insomnia, nervousness, cramps, heartburn. nausea, poor digestion. In large quantities peppermint is said to act as an aphrodisiac. Externally the leaves are used for their cooling qualities & to stop itching skin conditions.
Red Raspberry Leaf:	Leaves, fruit	Spring/ Summer	Used to reduce diarrhea & cramping. In tea form, it's used for menstrual problems (cramps, heavy blood flow) as an external wash for sores, wounds & skin rashes. Historically its taken by pregnant women to reduce miscarriage, reduce labor pain and increase milk.

Wolfen Wicca 2
Class #2
Herbal Baths and Herbal Bath Recipe

Herbal Baths are amazing! There's nothing like resting in the warm cozy water, as the healing properties of the herbs are infused into the water, and into your body. The wonderful scents of the oils surrounding you and penetrating all the corners of your mind.

Its an experience that you must try. Making herbal baths are very simple and easy. Here's what you do:

Take an approximately 8 inch square of cheese cloth or small holed netting and a string to tie it up with. Both of these can be purchased rather inexpensively, at any fabric store. I personally like using a drawstring muslin bag, about 3x5 inches, to put my herbal mixture in but its your preference.

Next choose the type of herbs you want to use in your bath sachet. Lay the ingredients in front of you and add the amount needed to your mixing bowl. **Do Not use metal of any type** in your herbs as it breaks down the inherent properties found in the herbs. Glass (is best), wood, or plastic is fine, just not metal. Mix the herbs with your fingers and hands. this allows the energies that you visualize pour out of your fingers and empower your herbal mixture.

Once the herbs have been mixed, you put the desired amount into the cloth or bag and tie up. If you're like me you always make way to much herbal mixture for just one sachet. So I just make up a few and store them in the fridge. Make sure what ever you store them in has a good seal, otherwise everything in the refrigerate will smell and taste like your sachets. I like using a glass jar with a screw lid, if you use plastic it often "takes on" the taste, smell of the sachets also. But again there's no exact right or wrong way, its up to you.

OK now all you need to do is draw your bath water, the hotter the better! You can hang the sachet over the facet so the water pours over it, as the water runs if you like.

Herbal Baths and Herbal Bath Recipe page 2

Then put the bath sachet into the hot water and let it steep, like a tea bag, for a few minutes. Then get in and relax. You can choose to leave the sachet in the water while you bathe, or take it out. Either way is fine, I like to leave mine in as it continues to release the herbal properties as I bathe.

Herbal Baths and Herbal Bath Recipe page 3

The following is a recipe for a herbal bath that works every time for me. Give it a try and let me know how it works for you.

Psychic Herbal Bath Recipe

(c) Lady Wolfen Mists 1978

This recipe is used to increase overall psychic energies. Use Once a week at least, daily is even better. To increase psychic abilities right before practicing them, bath in this herbal bath just prior to using the abilities.

- 3 drops Lilac Oil   (optional)
- 1 drop Rose Oil
- 3 parts Orange Peel
- 1 Part star Anise (whole is best)
- 2 broken Cinnamon Sticks
- 1 part Clove
- 3-4 parts Rose Petals

That's it , now mix, Visualize the goal or outcome you wish, put into cloth and tie up. Place in Bath and relax!!! Candles and soft music also help set the mood for your herbal bath. Hope it works as well for you as it does for me.

Wolfen Wicca 2
Class #2
Magickal Herbal Uses

The following are a few Magickal uses for Herbs. This is by no means meant to represent all there is, as volumes have been written on this subject, but it will give you a place to start from. It will allow you to experiment safely while you do your own personal research.

Astral Protection:	1. Mugwort, Poplar
Beauty:	Flax, Ginseng, Yerba Santa
Banishing:	Asafoetida, Birch, Dragons Blood, Clove, Juniper, Basil, Peach, Sandalwood, Mistletoe
Chastity:	Lavender, Vervain, Coconut
Courage:	Thyme, Yarrow, Sweetpea
Divination:	Cherry, Orris, Orange, Dandelion
Employment:	Jobs Tears, Buckeye, Lucky Hand, Pecan
Fertility:	Banana, Carrot, Cucumber, Dock, Hazel, Hawthorn
Fidelity:	Chickweed, Nutmeg, Clover, Elder
Friendships:	Lemon, Rose, Sweetpea

Happiness:	Catnip, Lilly of the Valley, Hawthorn, High John the Conqueror, Lavender
Hexes, To Break:	Bamboo, Poke, Thistle, Chili, Pepper, Wintergreen
Love, to Attract:,	Apple, Barley, Catnip, Chamomile, Cinnamon, Clover, Orange, Spearmint
Luck:	Aloe, Heather, Lilac, Jobs Tears, Lucky Hand
Lust, to create	Cat tail, Cinnamon, Dill, Vanilla, Violet, Clove, Musk, Spice
Luck, to Decrease:	Vervain, Camphor, Lettuce, Rosemary

Wolfen Wicca 2
Class #2
Cleansing Jars for Jar spells

© Lady Wolfen Mists 1990

Jar spells have a very ancient origin and are still practiced often today. They are simple to construct and usually very easy to do. They are inexpensive and can usually be done with items found in your home. There is, however a specific way of cleansing jars and other items to be used in this type of spell. This same procedure can be used for knot spells, but for our purpose we will focus on jar spellcasting.

The following gives steps on the cleansing procedure.

Items Needed;
    1 -bottle of Metaphysically Correct Holy water (See below for recipe)
    1 -jar
    Items to be used in the spell

Take all the items to be used in the spell and anoint them. To do this take a dab or two of Holy Water on your right index finger, and dab it onto the items to be used. Say the following;

> "<u>Item name</u> (i.e. stones, cord, jar) anointed by this water,
> Cleansed by all that's pure and positive.
> I consecrate you, <u>Item name</u>, to positive magicks
> and only positive works."

That's all there is to it. Once you have done this to all the items you will be using in a spell, you are ready to begin the spellcasting. You need only to d this once. However, you may do it at any time that you feel the items need to be reconsecrated. Cleansing helps to "set" the items with positive energies, and negates the negative ones that have been there. Cleansing also helps to ensure successful spellcasting. So even though it may take a few additional minutes, it's well worth your time and effort.

Wolfen Wicca 2
Class 2
Metaphysically Correct Holy Water

By Lady Wolfen Mists ©1982

An easy recipe for Metaphysically Correct Holy Water

1 quart	of Distilled water
3 drops	of Rose oil
3 to 6 drops	of Sweet Orange Oil
A pinch	of Hyssop in the water (optional)
1/2 teaspoon	of Glycerin (can get at any drug store)
A pinch of salt	(not to much, just enough to dissolve in water, sea salt is best but table salt will do)

Mix and shake. Place amount desired into Flask, that is to be used for this purpose only, and sprinkle around areas that the entity seems to be felt or seen around most often. Also sprinkle doorways and wipe, with cotton ball, around any openings to outdoors (windows, exhaust fans, OVER (not on) electrical plugs out lets, doggie doors, furnaces (wipe on the outside of the furnace) and so one.) Do this at least once a week, or as you feel the need, to maintain a "clean' house free of unwanted entities.

***Caution** remember this is oil and could cause stains on carpets and cloth so be careful when spraying if you are worried about the possibility of stains.) Any left over mixture can be stored in the 'fridge for about a week and 1/2 then you need to make a fresh batch.

I know this sounds really simple, I have been using it for many years, and it does work! I have had many satisfied customers using this simple but effective method! Let me know how it goes for you. Blessings, Lady Wolfen Mist

Lady Wolfen Mists

Wolfen Wicca 2
Class # 2
Practical: Making A Witches Wish Jar

Below is the general overall outline used for the practical section of this class. I've included this so if you have a specific question you can go directly to that section and find the answer quickly. I hope you find it helpful.

1. Purpose:
2. Items Included:
3. Special Information:
4. Steps to Preparation:
5. Special Storage Needs:
6. Clean Up:
7. Recharge Procedure

1)   This is a very old spell where you create an enchanted object to fill your wishes. There are two things you must remember in using this object, one is the **NEED VS GREED** rule. The second is that all wishes should start with the Phrase , "If it be in my Highest good and the Highest good of the Universe please let <u>(Whatever you wish)</u> occur." Then if its best for you and those around you the wish will be granted if not then it wont happen, no bad Karma to worry about!

Wolfen Wicca 2; Our Walk Onward To Initiation

Practical: Making A Witches Wish Jar page 2

2) Items Needed
    Sea weed   1-Jar with TIGHT sealing lid
    A pinch of Sea Salt   Enough Distilled water to fill jar
    1 Incense (stick)   Stick incense burner (holder)
                      Matches

3) Create this charm at night after dusk. Any moon phase. Once finished its ready for use.

4) **Steps**

1-- After Jar and items have been cleaned you need to open the jar and lay the lid to the side.

2.-- Add water to jar 3/4 of the way full.

3.-- Next pick up the Sea Weed and Hold it in your hands, close your eyes, feel its texture, smell it , inhaling deeply. You may take a small of it taste it if you like. It will be **VERY** salty. Visualize it as being from the original "Wishing Well", created by the Goddess and God, that place from where all life and wants began. See yourself becoming one with this great ocean of a well, see your wishes just floating and bobbing on the waves, waiting to be claimed by you. Visualize only those energies that allow for advancement to your spiritual quest being granted and filled.

4.-- Place sea weed into jar with water, you may tear the seaweed if its to big to fit in your jar, or only use part of the seaweed if there is to much.

5.-- Add additional water to the jar, leaving enough for a small amount of air at the top.

6.-- Now take a pinch or two of sea salt and add it to the mixture. This removes any negative energies that may have "slipped" by you in the construction if This spell.

7.-- Now Close the jar very tightly.

8.-- Light the stick incense and allow the smoke to fill the room for a minute or two.

Practical: Making A Witches Wish Jar page 3

9.-- Next take the completed, closed, jar and hold it out over the burning incense with both hands

10.-- Swirl the jar in a deosil direction 13 times, while holding it in both hands. Let the smoke from the incense flow over the jar and around it. While swirling the jar Visualize once more what you had already visualized in #3 above. Except this time "see" yourself IN the great ocean of wishes, swimming with the God and Goddess and all the wonders of their creation. "Know" that all they have made is only yours for the asking. Once this is done your jar spell is completed

5). **Storage & Use**
Store this item in the sunlight, I like placing it in the window. However this may pose a problem in the winter, I live in ND and it gets real cold and it could freeze, so you could put it in a shelf or table where it can get sunlight.

Use: It's real easy to use this item. Just pick it up and shake it up 3 times. Saying aloud once; "If it be in my Highest good and the Highest good of the Universe please let .(what you wish). occur." Then just put it back into the sunlight, know it will happen if it in your best interest.

6). **Clean Up**
Nothing special

7). **Recharge**
There is no recharge needed for this spell, as it contains Sea salt and Sea weed, it cleanses and repowers itself constantly. This item can be used for many many years to come. I've had one I made for well over 15 years now!

Notes on Class 2

Wolfen Wicca 2
Our Walk Onward To Initiation
Class #3

© Lady Wolfen Mists Jan.1990
revised 2001

Theory:
    Touching the Source of the Father
    Triple aspects of the God
    Hex Signs
    Traditional Color meanings Hex Signs
    List of God Names & Attributes

Practical:
    Ritual Healing For the Earth

Circle Work:
    What is your inspirational thought for the week.

Students in your Magickal Journal:
    Please answer the following questions. I would like you to explore the maleness in you and where it fits in Wicca.

(1) Is there an equal balance between the male and female part of you? (2) Do you need to work on that male part of you? (3) Is it too strong, overpowering your life? (4)Is it to weak, hidden afraid to be used? (5)What can you do to improve the balance? (6)Where, in your life and in your path of Wicca, do you see the male part of you working? (7)Are you satisfied where you are, concerning this subject? This will be reviewed when you submit your work for Initiation

"I Walk On!"

Wolfen Wicca 2
Class #3
Touching the source of the Father
Or Where He fits in Wicca

© Lady Wolfen Mists 1996

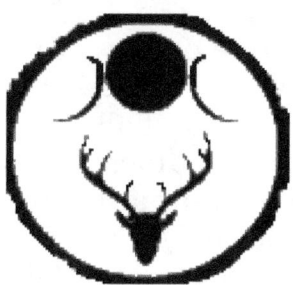

There often seems to be a misunderstanding concerning the role of the God in Wicca. Many practitioners push the God t the back of the picture, giving Him little importance and even less power. Others push Him to the front, ignoring the Goddess and devoting all there time to him and what power He has. To me either one of these extremes are wrong and out of the scope of what Wicca is about.

The God is always seen as next to the Bright Lady, not behind Her or below Her, but equal to Her side. This is vital in keeping the Balance and Harmony in the universe, it begins the polarity that is seen over and over in all aspects of life. That of negative and positive, not in the sense of good and bad, but in the sense that one is interdependent on the existence of the other. That is the way the God is seen to the Goddess, Her partner, different but essential to the existence of all.

She is the Dreamer, if you will, the idea. He is the force that brings things to their end. Without Him, as the activating force, much of life and the never ending circle would remain only an idea. He is the energy that activates the idea and brings it into the physical. It is true that She is the one who actually gives birth to the physical thing. Yet it needs to be understood that without the God's activating force, that birth would never have been conceived and thus in the end, No Creation! So with that in mind it is easy to see the importance of the God in Wicca, it is definitely not a passive role to be delegated to the back or a role that could be done alone. It is this interdependence on each other that sets the beauty of creation in motion, Balance in all things!

The God, like the Goddess, has many different roles that He is capable of fulling. Some of these roles have different names, different strengths that can be called upon. The idea of roles or aspects is not a difficult one to understand, but it can be confusing. So bare with me a second. Lets look at aspects and roles you may fill in your life.

Wolfen Wicca 2
Class #3
Touching the source of the Father
Or Where He fits in Wicca Page 2

© Lady Wolfen Mists 1996

You are someone's child (a role or aspect you fill), an employee (another role) and maybe a student or Father/Mother. These are all areas you work in, you have specific strengths in these areas that you call upon to successfully complete the job. However, even though you have many different aspects/ roles in your life, you are still YOU! Nothing can change that, no matter what other role/aspect you take on. This is very much the same with the God/dess. They are still the God/dess no matter what aspect you may call upon for help or understanding or worship. The God has as many aspects available to call upon as the Goddess. He can be seen for example, as a healer, a warrior, a consort (lover), a great Diviner, even as the inspiration of creation, just to name a few. He is as available to you as the Goddess, and you should never be hesitant to call on Him, when you feel the need.

Wolfen Wicca 2
Initiation Level
Class #3
Aspects of The God

© Lady Wolfen Mists Aug.5, 1996

The God, like the Goddess, has three (3) different aspects. His aspects correspond with the Sun and changes in the year. This chart gives an approximation of those times, and should not be considered the last word on this subject. Because the God corresponds to the sun, as the Goddess does to the moon, we can see the changes in His roles on a daily basis. Then, these same aspects can be seen in the greater scheme of things as the changes in the year progress.

God Aspect/role	Daily Sun time	Yearly correspondence
Youth	12:01 am- 8:00am	Spring/Summer
Warrior/ Father	8:01 am- 4:00 pm	Summer/ Winter
Sage/ Grandfather	4:01 pm-12:00am	Winter/Spring

These aspects should be considered when invoking a specific facet/aspect of the God. Just as you consider the phase of the moon and the aspect of the Goddess that most fits what you intend to do, so should you consider the Sun phase and the appropriate aspect of the God to be invoked.

Wolfen Wicca 2
Class #3
Hex Signs

© Lady Wolfen Mists 1996

Hex Signs are over 300 years old and were brought to the United States by the "Pennsylvania Dutch". These "Dutch" were actually from Germany, in the Rhine area, who mostly immigrated for religious freedom. These immigrants included the Amish and Mennonites (the plain dressed people) and the Lutheran and other Reformed groups (the Fancy dressed people). Coming from the middle to lower class, these working people were without much financial influence, but were rich in cultural traditions and customs.

One of theses customs/ traditions was the use of Hex Signs. Originally Hex Signs were called "Sech Circles" because they incorporated six sided stars into the designs. It was when the signs were brought to America they became commonly know as Hex Signs and the use of the name "Sech Circles" died away. Through the years they have had many different names including; Hexerie, Jinks, Witch Away's, and Blessings just to name a few. Yet no matter what one called them, they were used as powerful magickal tools, to be used with respect and humility.

Each Hex Sign consisted of a geometric design, that had been hand painted with very vivid and bright colors. It is interesting to note that although Witch Craft was considered evil and the work of the devil, the Hex signs were fully accepted by the "Fancy Dress" people. They were even encouraged , since they were said to bring blessings. But in my own opinion, Blessings or not, a spell is a spell! How could these strict religious followers tout evil and corruption on one hand, but goodness and "godliness" on the other, when in essence they were delving into the same behavior of those they condemned. But then if we had the answer to that we would be able

Class #3 Page 2
Hex Signs

to avoid many a religious wars and persecutions.

In any case the Hex signs in question, usually incorporated some type of central symbol in its over all design, like a unicorn or birds. These designs and colors had very specific meanings and reasons for their use within the Hex Sign. Some were to ward off bad luck, bring prosperity, stop fires, unhex curses, protection of family and belonging from evil, and on and on.

Today Hex Signs are few and far between, seen mostly on olden barns of days gone by. But lest we think that barns were the only place where hex signs were placed, we need to look again. Traditionally they were carved on furniture, Hope Chests, hammered into tools and painted on eating utensils, as well as on barns and homes. Just about anywhere one could be drawn, painted, placed or hammered, was considered an appropriate use of the signs. Looking at "pieces" from that period in history, we are amazed at where and how often we do find them in use.

In Wicca we can still use these wonderful signs as they were meant to be, as powerful symbols empowered by our own magickal ways. You can use the traditional symbols that have been passed down through the years or even create your own. Designed by you with personal reasons and symbols, empowered by you. Just be sure no matter what style you use, that you take time to "visualize" the attributes you want as you create the sign. Then when you have finished the actual creation process of painting, sanding, varnishing or whatever, be sure to consecrate you new Hex Sign. You can use a very elaborate ritual or simply use an oil Appropriate to what you are doing) and say your personal words of power. Then pass the Hex Sign through the ritual smoke (from the appropriate incense) to purify the Sign and to "set" the energies.

A note on the personal side. In my creation of Hex signs I like to incorporate a crystal or special stone. For instance I might put Black Obsidian, which is used to negate negativity, into my Hex Sign. I have also been known to use some of the Seals of Solomon to keep my house, car, locker, office, so on protected. I just take the picture and decoupage it on wood and paint colors over the symbols I

Class #3 Page 3
Hex Signs

can easily identify and make bright colors or white around the edges where it sits, gold is nice as well. As for repowering them I keep a monthly schedule, the full moon, letting them absorb their power from the fullness of the Mother, in the shining light of the Full moon. Using the full moon to cleanse and renew the energies within my Hex Sign also helps to remind me of the last time it was done! But, again it's all up to you as to how or even if you wish to cleanse and renew the energies with in the Sign. Remember there are no right and wrong ways of construction here, so have fun and experiment until you find a way that you feel suites you best.

Blessings,

Lady Wolfen Mists

Wolfen Wicca 2
Class #3
Traditional Color meanings for Hex Signs

© Lady Wolfen Mists 1996

Hex signs used on barns

Color:	Meaning
Gold	Financial Prosperity, Heaven
Red	Love, Passion, Protection from Lighting & Fire, Life lived well
Yellow	Sun, Truth, A child's (or children's) Purity, Holiness
Green	Prosperity in growth, Fertility, Abundance, Good Fortune & Luck
Blue	Protection from Physical, Natural Beauty, Tranquility, Spiritual
Violet/Purple	Power, Higher Protection from Spiritual persecution /Witchcraft
Brown	The Earth, Business works/agreements, sex, healthy harvest
White	Purity in the most High sense, White Light Protection, Happiness. Symbolizes the Creator (God, Goddess) Seasonal Harmony
Black	Lust (Sex in the negativity) Black Magic, Spiritual Possession, Hexing (cursed)

Lady Wolfen Mists

Wolfen Wicca 2
Class #3
List of God Names and Attributes

(G) = Greek Origin (E) = Egyptian Origin (C) = Celtic Origin
(R) = Roman Origin (N) = Norse Origin

<u>Adonis</u>	(G) God of beauty, love and vegetation
<u>Aesir</u>	(N) God of the seas
<u>Aeolus</u>	(G) God of winds
<u>Angus of the Brugh</u>	(C) God of youth
<u>Apollo</u>	(G) God of prophecy, music, medicine
<u>Arawn</u>	(C) God of the Underworld
<u>Artu</u>	(C) Wales God of hope, knowledge, justice. Warrior of people in distress & despair, unselfish love
<u>Balor</u>	(C) Kings of the Formorians, a hero and monster
<u>Beli</u>	(C) God of force, energy of the sun, fire, science

Wolfen Wicca 2; Our Walk Onward To Initiation

List of God Names and Attributes Page 2

<u>Boreas</u>	(G) God of wind (north)
<u>Bragi</u>	(N) God of poetry
<u>Cernunnos</u>	(C) Gaul God of all things wild & virility Horned God also mistakenly refereed to as Herne
<u>Consus</u>	(R) God of seed sowing
<u>Cupid</u>	(R) God of love
<u>Dagda</u>	(C) Irish God of Earth and all father
<u>Dian- Cecht</u>	(C) God of healing
<u>Dionysus</u>	(G) God of wine, vegetation, pleasure, civilization
<u>Dis Pater</u>	(R) God of Underworld
<u>Donar</u>	(N) God of thunder
<u>Eros</u>	(G) Go of love
<u>Faunus</u>	(R) God of crops, herds, oracular deity

Lady Wolfen Mists

List of God Names and Attributes Page 3

Februus	(R) God of underworld
Fides	(R) God of good faith
Ganymede	(G) God of rain
Genius	(R) God of protection of individuals, groups like a guardian Angel
Gwydion	(C) Welsh- Magician God This god conjured magick
Hades	(G) God of wealth & underworld
Heimdall	(N) "White god" guardian of Bridge Bifrost
Helios	(G) God of Sun
Hermes	(G) God of travelers, trade, eloquence
Hu	(C) God of harvest, growth, life, inspiration, future. "Laughing God" giver of fertility, commands the elements
Janus	(R) God of all types of doorways (portals) All things beginning & ending
Jupiter	(R) God of the sky
Keb	(E) God of Earth

List of God Names and Attributes Page 4

<u>Khensu</u>	(E) God of moon
<u>Lancelet (Lancelot)</u>	(C) This aspect of the God allows for the sacrifice of the normal to <u>Lancelot</u> a higher divine purpose, act of doing the higher idea
<u>Lar</u>	(R) God of the actual home, the protector
<u>Llugh</u>	(C) God of Justice, Supreme Will. He is the divine light, aids in all transitions of life, death & rebirth
<u>Loki</u>	(N) God of mischief
<u>Mac Lir</u>	(C) God of sea & fertility
<u>Manannan</u>	(C) God of sea & unconscious. He aids in resolving problems and coping with irrational fears
<u>Mars</u>	(R) God of war & agriculture
<u>Math</u>	(C) Wales - God of the underworld, enchantment, magick, teaching. He is known as a shape-changer
<u>Mathonny</u>	(C) Wales- God of sorcery
<u>Mercury</u>	(R) God of merchants
<u>Merlyn (Merlin)</u>	(C) Wales- God of mystery, healing, counseling, rituals, spellwork, <u>Merlin</u> magick & shape-shifting. When invoking be sure to understand that he has a strong belief in the law and will not bend

Lady Wolfen Mists

List of God Names and Attributes Page 5

Mithras	(R) God of regeneration
Moros	(G) God of destiny
Morpheus	(G) God of dreams
Neptune	(R) God of sea
Oceanus	(G) God of sea
Odin	(N) God of death, battle & inspiration
Ogmios (Ogma)	(C) God of eloquence, inspiration, language
Orcus	(R) God of death
Osiris	(E) God of life & death, symbolizes the yearly cycle
Pan	(G) God of herds, sexuality, lust
Pen Annwn	(C) God of the underworld
Poseidon	(G) God of the seas
Pwyll	(C) God of the Underworld, married the Goddess Rhiannon

List of God Names and Attributes Page 6

Ra   (E) God of the sun, all father figure for gods

Saturn   (R) God of workers and wine-growers

Sebek   (E) God of powers of darkness

Set   (E) God of evil & war, darkside of the God

Taliesin   (C) Wales- God of writing, poetry, music, magick, arts, crafts, wisdom, all knowledge, Bards. He's the force behind inspiration, the thought made manifest.

Thantos   (G) God of death

Thor   (N) God of thunder, sky, weather, crops

Thoth   (E) God of intelligence, learning, books, teaching

Tiwaz   (Germanic) God of battle, originally sky god concerned with law, justice, binding & solemn oaths

Vertumnus   (R) God of fruit & trees, a shape-shifter

Vulcan   (R) God of fire

Zeus   (G) God of all heaven, thunder and maker of all laws for mortals and gods

Wolfen Wicca 2
Class #3
Practical: Ritual For Healing the Earth

<u>By Lady Wolfen Mist © 09-03-1992</u>

The following ritual is set up for a group, but you can modify it for solitary use. This ritual can be performed at any moon phase as often as you like. The circle is cast and the altar is set up in the usual way. The grove tender/Fetch takes the ritual Cauldron and set it on the table, set up in the center of the circle, for this specific purpose. You can get flash paper at many costume supply stores if you can't find any just go ahead with out lighting the pentagram. I like the effect flash paper gives but its never necessary

High Priestess

"Tonight we gather to raise a cone of power to heal and cleanse our Mother. To do this we first add sacred salt of the sea."

(Grove Tender/Fetch hands Sea Salt to the High Priest)

Wolfen Wicca 2; Our Walk Onward To Initiation

Practical: Ritual For Healing the Earth Pg. 2

High Priest *(Adds Sea Salt at this time. Enough to lightly dust the bottom of the cauldron)*

"I add this purifier to the Earth Mother. May it boil and cleanse her negative, unclean energies."

High Priestess:

"I ask each of you to hold out the cup of Earth you have brought into our circle. Focus your energies and send these positive vibrations into your cups. Next, visualize these positive energies growing. See them building upon each other like a landslide, as they penetrate the Mother. "Feel" the negativity being overcome by positive healing powers! Do this now!"

All participants hold their cups out in front of themselves and visualize. When the cone of power has reached its "boiling over "state, the High Priest say the following:

High Priest:

"Children of the Mother! Come in perfect love and fill our cauldron with positive force and healing vibrations."

In a deosil manner all participants move forward one at a time toward the cauldron. The participant faces the north

Practical: Ritual For Healing the Earth Pg. 3

first, with a cup of Earth held over their heads by both hands. They walk 3 times around the cauldron saying the following once.

Individual Participant;

"From the Mother we come, To the Mother we return. Heal and cleanse her with these infused energies I send."

Then empty your cup of dirt into the cauldron. Place the empty jar/cup under the stand. Return to your place facing the altar. After all have added their energies and dirt, the High Priest adds his then the High Priestess adds hers.

The Grove Tender/Fetch hands a wooden stir stick to the High Priestess and a vial of holy water/Rose Water. The High Priestess takes them and pours/mixes them into the cauldron, The High Priest says the following as she adds the items;

High Priest:

"These sacred purifiers are added to seal our works. No longer will the Mother wince in pain as poison and sickness tear away at her. May this ritual cleanse and heal her."

The empty items are returned to the Grove Tender/Fetch who puts them away. The Grove Tender/Fetch hands the High Priestess the Pentacle, (the pentagram is wrapped with flash paper) and the lit taper from the altar.

Practical: Ritual For Healing the Earth Pg. 4

High Priestess: *(Lays or sticks pentagram into the cauldron)*

"We are the children of the old ways, we are keepers of the mysteries of life. We believe in death there is life, and in life there is love. Death is a balance to life. Illness a balance to health **LET THE BALANCE BE STRUCK!** Let the Mother who has suffered be healed. Let our energies direct our love and wisdom. We invoke our most protective sign, for our Mother. LET IT BE SO!"

(High Priestess lights the Pentagram)

All Say:

"**Blessed Be to all, May the Mother be Healed. May our energies be infused in this Earth. Let the balance be struck!**"

The High Priestess now opens the circle for all to express their feelings. When the rite is completed it is banished as usual. The cauldron can be emptied in one place outside or each person can take some home. They then can return it to the place they got it from, so that the energies can be spread to all corners.

Notes on your Practical

Notes on Class 3

Wolfen Wicca 2
Our Walk Onward To Initiation
Class #4

© Lady Wolfen Mists Jan.1990
revised 2001

Theory:
    Reincarnation
    Karma general overview
    Karma Wolfen Wicca View
    Perfect Love & Trust: What it means
    Honor
    Uncross and Send Back

Practical:
    Past Life Guided Experience

Circle Work:
    What is your inspirational thought for the week.

***Assignment:

Students in your Magickal Journal: Please relate how your past life guided experience went. Give as much information and details as you feel comfortable with. Where did you return to? Where there people there then that are in your life now? Were you male or female? Is there a specific cycle or lesson that you are learning in this lifetime that connects to this past life. This will be reviewed when you submit your work for Initiation ☺

"I Walk On!"

Wolfen Wicca 2
Class #4
A bit on Reincarnation
© By Lady Wolfen Mists 1990

As you already know Wicca is a very individual religion, so it is next to impossible to include for every Wiccan idea/thought in the community. Because of this there are no "hard and fast rules" when it comes to doctrine or Traditions or paths. As such it become very difficult to teach what is the Wiccan way concerning personal beliefs in various area. So what I am giving to you here is my personal belief system, and the one I have found to be most common when speaking to others of my faith. However I do not want to leave you with the misguided impression that this is by any means the only way or the final answer. There are others who's beliefs may vary from this in minuet ways to large jumps and gaps. Each are considered acceptable and "right" for that individual. The few basic items that it seems all of us adhere to is a strong belief in the <u>Wiccan Rede</u> (...Harm Ye None) and the <u>Three (3) fold law</u>.

What is reincarnation? How does it work? Why reincarnate at all? Is it always on this plane of existence? Do animals reincarnate? What happens when you die? Where do you go? These are all questions that have been asked by students and seekers for centuries. The answers are often subjective to the individual but I will attempt to answer them as best I can. Hopefully with this knowledge, you will be able to construct your own opinions on these ancient subjects.

Reincarnation is simply the rebirth of you from your Higher Self, in an attempt to learn specific lessons, and gain knowledge. This knowledge allows us on the non-physical or spiritual plane to ascend to higher realms and other realities. In Wicca we believe in

Lady Wolfen Mists

Wolfen Wicca 2
Class #4
A bit on Reincarnation 2

something termed "progressive reincarnation." Pretty impressive sounding isn't it? What it really means is fairly simple:

1. We return to this plane or consciousness as always Human. We return in unisex roles, meaning in one life you may be female and male in yet another.

2. Each lifetime holds obstacles as well as opportunities that allow us to evolve in a positive way. We have conscious knowledge of the choices we make, be they positive or negative in nature. As such we are consciously responsible for the way we live and grow in our lifetimes.

3. We believe that each life, in some way is better that the last. If it is nothing more than being more aware of your spiritual quest (as if that isn't enough)

4. Most Wiccans also believe that the quality of your "Life" is equal to the learning experience agreed upon. This agreement was made by you, prior to your incarnation. You decide what it is you are to "Learn" in this lifetime and what type of life you will provide or live to learn these lessons.

So that's what that impressive term "Progressive reincarnation" means. With it you begin the foundation to answering these age old questions. But now you want to know, if we believe in reincarnation what happens when we die. We believe in a soul/spirit that returns to a higher realm of existence. We do not believe in the concept of Heaven for some and Hell for others. Our Lady and Lord gives us unconditional love and wonderful acceptance, no matter how long it takes us to get our lessons finished. When you die or "cross" your soul/spirit returns to the place it first came from. In our case we call this , "The Summer Land". The Summer Land can be likened to a very busy bus station, everyone with a spirit/soul goes through here, some go up to a higher place or another dimension, some return to the physical plane. But what this means is that everyone truly everyone, those kind and generous in their lifetime as well as those who were not, every soul returns here. When you first return to the Summer Land, traditionally though to be located somewhere in the East, you are met by other souls/spirits that meant something to you in your last life. They welcome you to this wonderful land and they may spend a short time with you. You are then met by The Bright Lady and Lord and your contract, the agreement you made prior to this, is pulled out. Now don't get the wrong idea, there is no one who keeps a list of "rights and wrongs" you committed while living on earth. However your life is reviewed and the lessons that you wanted to learn are looked at, you consider and judge how well you performed, and whether you need to learn that lesson again or not. For example you wanted to learn the lesson of compassion. You see yourself in a scene in you past recent life where you could have experienced this.

Wolfen Wicca 2
Class #4
A bit on Reincarnation 3

Maybe a homeless person needed help or food. You were busy, maybe late for work. Did you stop and lend a hand or did you turn your back and think, "why don't they just get a job?" If you took the time to help them then you successfully learned that lesson, if you walked away, that may be a lesson you chose to try and learn again in yet another life. But the point is no one but you decides, the Lord and lady may talk with you about your actions but you make the final decision. You may even become aware of cycles in your life where you could have learned that lesson again and again, but failed to grasp the idea. This often explains cycles seen in our every daylives, lessons waiting to be completed successfully. With the opportunity given again and again, as many times as needed, for us to "get it right"

OK, so now you've gone over your contract. You feel you did pretty good on some things, not so good on others. Now you decide what lessons you will learn on your next return. You make that contract with the Lady and Lord and put it away. With all that out of the way you are free to enjoy the Summer Land as long as you wish. Its a place of wonder, where you can relax, rest and recuperate. Spend time with friends and make new ones, (maybe even find a soul group you will incarnate with again and again).When the time draw near for you to decide to return to you "studies" you prepare yourself, looking for the situation you wish to be born into, one that will give you the most opportunities to successfully learn the lessons you have decided upon. Once that is found your spirit/soul re-enters the physical plane and you are reborn, or reincarnated, without any conscious memories of your time at the Summer Land. One other item concerning the Summer Land I want to make before we move on is an answer to the question, "Do animals go to the Summer Land & o they reincarnate also?" My answer to both is a very emphatic "Yes". Animals have a spirit/soul also. How can you look into the eyes of your dog or cat or horse or any creature and not see and feel the love there, the intelligence, the attachment to you at the soul level? If the Summer Land has every soul returning there at "cross over times" then animals must be there also. As to whether they re-incarnate or not, I feel they do. Animals have lessons that they learn on their spiritual journey as well as we do. They are a wonder of creation just as we are, I find it impossible to believe that the Lord and Lady would create such wonders of love and only give them a "one shot deal" to get it right. Summer Land is as much for other life forms, be they something we are familiar with or not, as it is for the ascension of human kind. Anyway that's what I feel and that is the basic tenet in Wolfen Wicca ®.

Blessings,
Lady Wolfen Mists

Wolfen Wicca 2
Class #4
A bit on Karma In General

© By Lady Wolfen Mists 1989

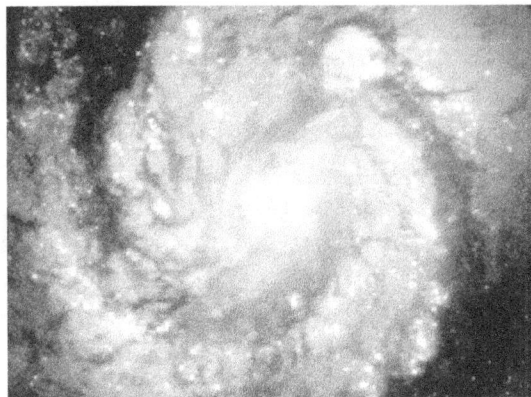

Karma is another one of those ideas that is hard to pin down because there are so many approaches to the concept. As well as there being no real hard and fast rules, each sect is allowed to interpret Karma (also called The LAW of RETURN) as befits that sects basic belief system. Yet the most popular version states that for every negative action we make, we must receive a negative action in return. Similarly, for every positive action, we must receive a positive action. A negative action, being one that stops or inhibits our spiritual growth. A positive action is seen as one that aids or directs our spiritual growth to a higher realm of existence.

The Law of Return (karma) is set in the precept that the universe must pay us for every act we commit, making us responsible for all our actions. Also making us responsible for our own personal harmony and balance as well as aiding to the Harmony and balance of the word and thus the universe.

For those of you into the more scientific approach, think of Karma as conforming to Newtons Physics and the laws found therein. The universe is seen as one huge machine that's end results are completely predictable. The predictability is in the "workings" of the machine, that the gears and pulleys interact upon one another, each cause and effect, generating a predictable outcome. This machine (interaction and interdependence) continues until one day, when the cause and effect reach the end of the gear system, or the machine runs out of gas. Then the machine stops (another predictable end result) and Karma (as we understand it) stops!

But how do practitioners of the craft in general view Karma? We see karma as justice. It allows for the explanation of why negative people or actions happen in this world. Why these people or actions seems to get away "free and clear" with this type of behavior. We know that at some point in a future lifetime they MUST repay their actions, in the Law of Return. They are locked into a repayment and can not avoid it for that is how the Universe works!

Wolfen Wicca 2; Our Walk Onward To Initiation

A bit on Karma in General Page 2

Members of the Craft (and others) almost always have questions on "Karmic Ties"to other beings. Do we have beings/souls that we incarnate with over and over again? This is another individual answer that varies for each person. However, I know you want some other type of answer than that so, I will give you my beliefs on this issue.

It has been my experience that there are most certainly a specific group of souls that you incarnate with, over the many lifetime. I have collected this knowledge, over the years, from my training in the Craft. By viewing my own past lives and how they interacted with the people around me, and listening to how these same people explain their own past lives. From there I learned to see and identify the Karmic patterns of these interactions in the everyday life around me. From this I learned that this specific group of souls, or beings, are known as your personal soul group. It is from this group that your soul mate is found!

Say as long as we are speaking of soul mates let me stray for a second and explain this term as I see and understand it. Soul mate is a term that has been overused by those New Age Money Makers and never truly explained. A soul mate is someone that you have spent many many lifetimes with, that helps complete you as a whole. The opposite half of you. There is no ONE and only soul mate for you. I know that's a wonderful romantic notion but it just a notion. Your Soul mate comes from your Soul Group, as there are many in this group, there are quite a few to choose from. So if you lose (IE. through death) or miss (IE. just never connect) your soul mate you can still have that deep loving experience by finding another member of your Soul Group that fits your needs. This explains why you can feel a deep connection to more than one mate/being in your lifetime.

But back to the topic Soul Group. It is also this Soul Group that you grow with and experience the many lessons that one must learn before one can ascend to a Higher Realm of existence. I hope this helps you somewhat in your understanding of Karma and Soul Groups. Please remember that there is no ONE answer and if you find yourself saying, "I cant Buy all that she said" that's OK, because I want you to think for yourself and find your own answers. After all who better can develop YOUR magick system, than you. I am here as a guide, not as the one & only, final word. If you find that you can accept my explanation, then that's OK too. You have listened, read , thought and decided what is acceptable to your system of Magick. It may or may not change as you add your own personal experience, but that is the beauty of the Craft, it allows for growth!

Blessings,
Lady Wolfen Mists

The Universe is an Amazing Place

Wolfen Wicca 2
Class # 4
KARMA- How it works in Wolfen Wicca

© Lady Wolfen Mists 2001

This is not a rant, its more of an explanation of our (Wolfen Wicca) understanding of Karma and how it works in our life. Many of you have written about Karma and seem to have a slight misunderstanding of how it works. Admittedly karma has become one of those new age buzz words that are never really explained or defined just used a lot. So I felt it was important for **my** students to have a good grasp of its meaning (from our perspective) and maybe help anyone else who would like a little more understanding of the Word.

First off it should be noted that Karma is not originally a Wiccan idea it comes more from the Hindu belief system and has been adopted by many other spiritual traditions. The general belief of Karma is that all actions (and <u>not doing</u> something is considered an action, as well as doing something) cause results/consequences in the grand scheme of things. As the universe runs in harmony and balance, and you are part of that universe, every single thing that you do cause ripples in the universal energies. As a result, you develop karma for everything you do. **Karma is the consequences of your actions.** Some karma is more traumatic or apparent than others for example you kill someone, the consequence may be in the next life time they exact justice from you and cause you great pain, thus equaling out the balance of energies. Another less apparent karmic bond may be that you save a kitten from getting run over. In another life (or maybe in this lifetime) you develop a strong loyal bond with a kitten and it may even save your life in some way.

So Karma simply put, is the result of previous acts or deeds, either in the past or in past lives. The Law of Return (karma) is set in the precept that the universe must pay us for every act we commit, making us responsible for all our actions and keeping a balance in energies. This makes us responsible for our own personal harmony and balance as well as aiding to the Harmony and balance of the world and thus the universe.

Karma Gets a bad Rap

Karma often gets a bad rap because most everyone assumes that karma is only negative and that negative consequences are being developed. While there are negative aspects that you must repay as consequences of actions there are also positive ones. You can gain positive karma for all the good things you do and all the events/situations you help others with. Karma builds for positive just as swiftly as negative and such positive results are often overlooked by many. The universe must keep in balance al things and positive is just as powerful as negative, repayment is just as eminent and even more welcome. So don't get stuck on seeing karma as just bad there's plenty of good karma out there too.

The Karma Bank

The misunderstanding of Karma usually comes in the idea of a Karma Bank. Many Westerners misinterpret the idea of building up Karma. They believe that by doing a positive act, they cancel or erase a negative act. They think they can set aside or attempt to build up their "karmic bank account" with positive actions, so as to allow or make up for any negative actions they may have done or do in the future. **This just isn't the way it works!** If you do something negative to someone, the universe will at some point, either in this lifetime or another, deal the same situation out to you that you did to another. **It doesn't matter how many other positive things you many have done, you still gotta pay for the negativity you caused.** This sounds kinda doom and gloomy but The Law of Return works the same way for positive actions! Any positive action you give out must be returned to you in full, either in this lifetime or another. So there is no banking Karma to allow for "slip ups" Doing harm to another results in the consequence of you feeling that harm at another time. Doing good for another results in you experiencing good at another time also. You are the one solely responsible for your choices.

Helping Karma Move

We have all heard the saying "just a little bit of karma coming down" or even someone say they are just helping Karma move a bit faster. Well sorry to say its not up to you when, where and if Karma happens. Its is up to the universe, in the awesomeness of the universe it knows when a person is ready to pay back karma and

Wolfen Wicca 2; Our Walk Onward To Initiation

KARMA- How it works in Wolfen Wicca page 3

when to collect the dues (energies) needed to balance what has gone on before. To pretend that you are an agent of such remedies is just plain silly and does nothing but build negative karma for you as you inflict pain on others. Of course its your choice and you will be the one to pay, good or bad its up to you. You can invoke the 3 fold law but that's another whole kettle of fish ;-)

Have faith in the Universe and know that all things come out in the wash and all things are balanced eventually.

But how do practitioners of the craft view Karma?

We see karma as universal justice. It allows for the explanation of why negative people or actions happen in this world. Why these people or actions seems to get away "free and clear" with this type of behavior. We know that at some point in a future lifetime they MUST repay their actions, in the Law of Return. They are locked into a repayment and can not avoid it for that is how the Universe works!

Conclusion

So there you have it in a nutshell, I hope this helps in your understanding. If you have any other questions please ask and I'll do my best to answer. I don't claim to have all the answers but I sure will be happy to share what I do know with you :-)

Addendum

I thought I had covered every thing on karma until I read this which lead to this addendum. Here's the question:

Whilst having dinner with two friends one night, we got to talking about Karmic twists. Here's a thought that occurred to me after the fact. *Children: Is one automatically involved in the Karma of their children simply by giving them life? Or, do parents really only provide the vessel for the child/ spirit to live in throughout their physical life?*

The answer to this may be a bit hard to grasp but I will try to make it as understandable as my meager words allow. When one decides to have children then one takes on the responsibility of that child's growing nurturing needs. You are its guide on all levels, you teach it the ways of life and compassion and humanity, the lighted soul lifting path. It is <u>here that karma becomes a part of the child and your cycle</u>, what you teach the child. What you do or do not give it in respect to its physical, emotional and spiritual needs. If you, as the caretaker and guide of this child, do not do your job in a proper manner (teaching it fully as best you can and know how to do) then you are tied by karmic deeds to this child until you fulfill your end of the agreement.

The agreement being to guide and nurture this child in some positive manner, that may be with your own hands or seeing that this child is placed in a home where such as guidance and nurturing of body mind & soul is available for a life time. You

KARMA- How it works in Wolfen Wicca page 4

have a responsibility to this life that is totally and <u>100% dependent on you</u> and your decisions.

However as the child grows and you teach it (morals, values, spiritual, emotional and physical sustenance) then the child begins to make its own decisions. This is their own karma, and you may or may not be involved in this, as you gave them the tools to make good (positive) decisions and how they choose to use that information is now laid at their doorstep alone.

Now you as a parent <u>can lock yourself in to a child's karma</u> (often in a negative way) by not allowing them to grow and take responsibility for the decisions they make. As a parent you rush to their side to "make it all better" and in such a case interfere with the lesson being learned and the karma (positive or negative) being built. Creating a karmic circle that becomes hard to break in a lifetime by both sides.

A more positive approach would be to go to them and tell them you love them no matter what but that they must "own up" to the deed (responsibility & balance in all things) they did and live through the consequences of that deed. This is not only more loving in nature but better in the long run, as the lesson needing to be learned is often learned the first or second time on their own. As opposed to you "fixing it" and getting all mixed up in karma and lessons that you weren't meant to be in. This action of being involved when you shouldn't be could end in the child having to re learn the lesson down the road in a much harder and more painful manner. As hard as it is to sit and watch people you love make "dumb decisions" (which you could easily fix) it is their life and they must learn to live it. We must respect their choices (as they grow) and allow them to experience the results, this is life experience and it is a great teacher of wisdom.

So yes, you as a parent are connected to a child by karma, you are its teacher all through its life. First as the one who feeds and clothes and teaches about life, your decisions create the Karmic bond here 100 %. Later as a parent who allows and trusts what they have taught the child. You allow the child to make decisions as much as possible. You guide when asked, you respect them as a growing person to make decisions about their life. You **always nurture** the soul to reach for the lighted path and you allow the child to deal with the results of their own decisions as they build not only their own life experience but their own karma outside of yours.

You will always be their parent, you will always love them deeply as they are a part of you, but do you trust yourself and your teachings enough (as well as the Lady and Lord) to know that you did the best you could and the child can now stand on its own 2 feet with out making all the decisions for them?

KARMA- How it works in Wolfen Wicca page 5

Karma is balance and responsibility and consequences (both positive and negative) of all situations. Allow you child to build their own balance and to include you in a positive way and not in a manner that stifles the growth of everyone involved.

OK so that should cove about all I can think of in the Wolfen Wicca perspective of Karma. Hope it helps make things a little clearer.

Blessings,
LWM

Lady Wolfen Mists

Wolfen Wicca 2
Class # 4
Perfect Love & Perfect Trust

© LWM June 29th 2007

Let us talk about perfect love and perfect trust. These terms are flung about in Wicca often with out a second thought. Such things as how do you come to the circle to worship? The answer is *"In Perfect Love and Perfect Trust."* When speaking of the coven it is almost always in perfect love and perfect trust. Yet what do those words really mean?

Many think that it means that you must have perfect love and perfect trust for every single person within your coven/grove or within the pagan community. Now come on, I don't know about you but I personally am a very flawed human being and anything in perfection is a bit beyond me. I can do good, I can even do very good, I can try my best, but perfection...hum I just don't know about that.

The Goddess and God who knows we are not perfect would not expect such standards from us now would They? They would never set us up for failure and

Wolfen Wicca 2; Our Walk Onward To Initiation

Perfect Love & Perfect Trust Page 2

standards from us now would They? They would never set us up for failure and unattainable results. For it is true we all have personalities and feelings and emotions and someone at sometime is gonna brush someone else the wrong way. Whether this is an intentional act or not, the sheer fact of being hurt or aggravated or plain feed up with another throws perfect love and trust within the circle, out the window. So what could the Goddess and God really want from us that we could possible deliver to them over and over?

In my experience (notice I said my experience for it is the Bright Lady and Lord who told me this years ago in an astral journey.) I have found that the perfect love and trust is not for others in my circle but for the Lady and Lord Themselves. That I come with this perfect love and perfect trust for Them in my heart. That I know no matter what happens, no matter who hurts or upsets me it is all going to work out for the best, as it is within the sight and hands of my Bright Lord and Lady. That if I respectfully cleanse my heart, mind and soul, when I enter this circle and I replace mundane thoughts with worship and Perfect Love and Perfect Trust for the words and actions of the Lady and Lord all the rest falls into place. In as much I will see the divine spark of the Bright Ones in the heart and soul of each member beside me. Therefore I will reflect that Perfect Love and Perfect Trust to the Divine spark each member possess.

For that reason there is no need for me to have to love everyone before I enter the circle, no need to trust completely those about me (yet it is nice if I can do this but it is not necessary.) For when I come together in a sacred place it is to the Lady and Lord I come to, bearing my open soul and doing so in <u>sublime submission</u> to Their wants and practices. I give to Them over and over my most Perfect Love and Perfect Trust. Consequently it radiates to all those about me in a loving manner, causing all involved to act within their higher self and exercising the very highest intent of all, which is to be as one with the Lady and Lord of Light.

So next time you hear the words "In Perfect Love and Perfect Trust" <u>**really think on them.**</u> Then reflect that in your human form you are trying the best you can. That you are delivering to the Lady and Lord the most sacred gift of Love and Trust in all its divine Perfection to all aspects of Them that you see, even those other humans beside you who you may not feel the most sure with. This my friends is truly Perfect Love and Perfect Trust!

Many Blessings,
Lady Wolfen Mists

Wolfen Wicca 2
Class # 4
On Honor

© Lady Wolfen Mists 2001

Dear Ones, come gather around our bonfire and let us tonight talk about Honor. I have defined Honor for your purposes as the following (taken from merriam-webster dictionary a: good name or public esteem : reputation b: a showing of usually merited respect : recognition <pay *honor* to our founder> a: a keen sense of ethical conduct : integrity <wouldn't do it as a matter of *honor*> b: one's word given as a guarantee of performance <on my *honor*, I will be there>

I have tried as best I can to live a life of honor, to make my word worthwhile and to do what is true and right and correct, even if it costs me something which was rightfully mine, I still do my best to do what is honorable. That's not to say I haven't made mistakes. I am human and mistakes happen but I do do my best to try and keep a life of honor. Yet I have found that many people take advantage of those who try to live in honor. In today's "civilized" world such concepts seem old, decayed and outdated. Most take what is offered without regard to if taking what is offered it right and true and correct.

They live a life of what they think they can get, what they deserve because poor them were wronged, and someone is gonna pay, and they don't care who! A life not really based on what they know is the true and correct thing to do.

Its kinda like that song *The night they drove ol' Dixie down*
"But they should never have taken the very best." Just because it's offered, just **because you can do it** , doesn't mean it's the honorable thing to do. Why has this

On Honor Page 2

become such a foreign notion in our lives? Why must I even address this? Why is this not taught to us as children and ingrained on our hearts as the knights of old did. I am not sure why it is this way today. Is it our need to have? Our drive to constantly to be one up on those around us? Is it just because we don't care and the one with the most toys wins...again I don't know but I do know I have seen it in the lives of oh so many about me.

People who really had nothing to do with the act that was done (the wrong done.) Yet because the one with honor felt some responsibility they <u>offered what they truly didn't have</u>, and it was quickly gluttoned up by the one who felt wronged.

Perhaps this is too esoteric to follow, lets make it simple. Say someone you knew (person A) was hurt by someone else (person B) you introduced them to. The act cost person A some unexpected cash, you know person B can't pay it but you feel something should be done. You have a very limited amount of cash but you eke out an amount to offer person A because you feel that there is some responsibility due to your introducing them. Now it is well known you are in a very bad way yourself, little to no income and loss of all you have; yet you take your last few pennies and offer them. It sets you way back...**but in honor the offer must be made**.

You do it, person A quickly agrees to take your offer, no matter it was not truly your fault. This person takes from you even though they know you are broke and trying to do the right thing. There is little if any thought as to if this will harm you, there is little respect that this offer was one made in honor. That such an offer should be denied but told that the thought was deeply appreciated.

That just because the offer was made and that person A could do it, they truly should not, for their acceptance is not an honorable act in and of itself. *("But they should never have taken the very best.")* <u>At the very most</u> person A should have taken only some, but not all, of the offer.

In the Asian culture items that are admired are often offered to the person who admires it. Yet the person who admires **it knows better than to take it (such an act would be an insult and dishonorable.)** Instead they thank the person profusely and of course leave the item in the care of the family it comes from. This is Politeness, Honor, Integrity and Respect.

So I ask you Dear Ones, where are you in taking what is offered? Where are you in living a life of Honor, and respect for others? Do you take just because it will make your life easier and the hell with the one offering? Do you always take it all, take the very best? Is this HONOR? Do you instead say, "Thank you for caring and your kind offer, but it will be OK?"

On Honor Page 3

  Now don't get me wrong taking help and asking for it is one thing…its OK and something you should do. But taking just because you can and taking the best is WRONG. Taking when you know it will cause the other one who offered to suffer is wrong. **THINK my friends, THINK!** Because no matter what you say, no matter how you justify it wrong is wrong and not a life lived in honor. What kinda life do you live?

  As Children of the Lady and Lord of Light we should try to live a life of Integrity, Respect, Compassion and Honor. If nothing else in your path please please carve this into your heart, mind and soul, have your actions show this and do your best act in honor. Love each other, care for each other, respect each other for we must remember that **PEOPLE ARE ALWAYS MORE IMPORTANT THAN THINGS!** Period!!!!

"Honor is found within, look to your inner wolf to guide you when in Doubt"

Wolfen Wicca 2
Class # 4
To Uncross & Send Back Spell

© By Lady Wolfen Mists 5-1992 revised 1999

Items Needed:
1 --Black Image candle of your sex
1 --White Image Candle of your sex
1 --Green Taper
1 --Goddess oil for dressing candle
1 --Yellow taper
1 --Red Taper
1 --Blue Taper
1 --Bag Black Salt

This spell is used to unhex you from anything that may have been sent your way. In addition to that, it will also send it back to its original sender. It can be cast at any moon phase.

Dress the candles with Moon Water Oil oil. "See" the white candle symbolizing you. "See" the black image candle symbolizing the negative energies around. The four (4) other candles around you represent the elements that will aid in protecting you.

To begin, place the black image candle in the center of the altar with the white one directly behind it. Put the four (4) element candles in their appropriate places. Remember to keep them five (5)- six (6) inches away from the center candles. If you are unsure of the directions of the elements here are their placements. Green above the center (white) candle. Yellow to the right of the center candles. Red below the center candles. Blue tot he left of the center candles.

Now light all the candles, white first. Then the green and so on in a clockwise, deosil, manner. Light the black image candle last. Now say the following.

**"May all the elements burn and see,
all those who have crossed me,
All who have meant to bring harm to me.
Now comes the time,
To return in kind.**

To Uncross & Send Back page 2

**Three times stronger I send it to thee,
All of your evil and negativity!'**

Wait ten (10) heartbeats as the candles burn. Visualize all the negative energies that you wish to turn back, being absorbed by the black candle. Now move the candle out to the left, beyond the blue candle. Wait three (13) heartbeats. Visualize the white candle being clean and protected. "See" a barrier put up by the elements that only allow positive energies through to you. Now say the following;

**"I'm sending it back and putting it away.
I send it to your house and there it will stay.
Never again to darken my door
Now that it's over I've settled the score."**

Let the candles continue to burn for twenty (20)--twenty five (25) minutes. Then snuff them out and say:

"The Three fold law has been invoked. So Mote It Be!"

In the clean up place the black image candle in a bag (brown lunch bags work fine) and put the black sand in it. Then put it in the trash (Kitty litter works great here)and don't bother it again. Next put the white image candle in another bag, make sure the bag is clean, and put white sea salt (or table salt) in it. Place this in the trash also. The four (4) element candles can be saved, if you wish, and used again. Or you can put these in the trash also.

Lady Wolfen Mists

Wolfen Wicca 2
Class # 4
Practical Past Life Regression

© Lady Wolfen Mists 1990 revised 1992, 2001

Reason For:

To Determine if there are people in your present day life that you have had past life connections with. Please use Kitaro *Light Of The Spirit* CD from the 101 class if you have it for this pathworking.

Greeting and welcome, we are about to take a journey into your inner self, your subconscious. We will be looking to find people who are in your present day life that were also in a past life, these people must have made positive contributions in your past life, so we will be looking for an overall positive experience.

I am a Certified Hypnotherapist but we will not be using hypnosis here. Instead we will be using a guided experience that allows for memory recall, I have used this same process many times over and have always had profound success with it. Don't worry, just let the images flow, don't try to figure them out or analyze them, just allow them. You will want to record this script first so you can listen to it when you are ready to give it a try. Be sure to give few seconds between each instruction to allow you time to do it. Don't worry if you have to do it a few times, it takes time to learn to relax and let the images come forward

Before you begin the actual exercise there are a few things you will need to do, first remove any restrictive clothing. If your clothes are to tight or rub you they may interfere with your ability to relax.

Second GO to the BATHROOM! There's nothing worse then getting half way through this and then your brain telling you you gotta pee.

Third remove any glasses or watches from your body and put in a safe place. OK Go do that now.

Now that you are back get ready to go. Take the phone off the hook and find a place that's quite, where you can lay down and not be

Wolfen Wicca 2; Our Walk Onward To Initiation

Practical Past Life Regression Page 2

disturbed. Now Lay down, you might want to place a blanket across you, as your body temperature will drop somewhat. Don't cross your legs and if possible lay your hands to your sides. However what's really important here is that you are in a comfortable position. now close your eyes and listen to your voice on the recording and the instructions.

Exercise:
1. Begin your 4 count breathing, allow the air to flow in and out. Become aware of the filling of your lungs, the feeling of exhaling

2. Allow you entire body to relax

Start at head and move down to feet—Give enough time to actually feel the relaxation

3. Once totally relaxed see a cave and move into it. There are torches on the walls and a set of 10 steps. each step going down puts you in a more and more relaxed state.

Lets begin
    10...9...8...moving down, moving down

    7.. 6.. 5...half way to the bottom and feeling very very heavy,

    4.. 3... you are so tired and heavy, your legs feel like poles of steel and still you move down

    2... Down 1...and 0

At the bottom of the stairs is a large bed of cool moss, you fall safely into it, it surrounds you and tucks you in its warm cocoon. You are more relaxed at this point then you have ever been before.

4. Your body will continue to safely/fully function as it does in this time/space continuum in <u>(Year)</u>

*. You will continue to breath, swallow, and retain full bladder control through out this session, no matter where or when your past life takes you. You will also be able to express yourself in English No matter what language your past life may be

*You will be in complete control of all body functions and should an emergency arise in this room you will find that you will awaken and be able to handle the situation fully awake and in a successful manner.

*If at any time the regression becomes to painful for you, you may stop or continue through the pain as an observer. If the information that you collect at this session should be to painful or hard for you to handle in your present physical lifetime, your subconscious will store that information, until such a time you can successfully deal with the information collected with a MINIMUM amount of pain.

5. You will feel your spirit becoming very light and rising out of your physical body, just hanging,....floating in the air. You may feel yourself moving back through your current physical lifetime. You may see pictures or scenes from you life. Don't take time to try and understand anything happening or going on, Just go with the flow and allow it to happen. Later you can analyze it all you like, now just continue to move back, further and further, moving back, moving back.

6. While you are seeing these scenes, you may view them much as you would a video. These things have already happened and you feel no pain or emotions to what you are seeing.

   If you feel anything, feel confident that these emotions can in no way harm you. You have been there before and are completely safe now.

7. Lifting out of the body and drifting, allowing your subconscious to find a past life where you and another were together in a positive helpful experience. See that life becoming aware of the things going on about you. Be open to the images as they come to you, just allow these pictures, feeling, smells, sounds to flow and through you.

Practical Past Life Regression Page 4

8. Begin to become more aware of that special lifetime, and begin to drift down into that item. Slowly allowing yourself to settle in.

9. As you settle in this world and time should begin to become ,more focused. Becoming more and more clear. Slowly clearer and clearer. The feeling stronger and stronger.

10. At this time things should be completely clear and vivid. Remember to remain confident that this has already happened and nothing can harm you in any way. However if things become to difficult for you to see or experience you can fast forward, like a video past that point. You can move, explore read, talk and hear. You are in complete control of this past life experience. Go and explore now.

11. Here may be a few things you wish to notice.
    *What are you wearing? How do they look?
    *Is there a mirror or still water you can see your own reflection in?
    * What do you see?
    *Who is the person you recognize that appears in both the present and past life?
    *What is it in the past that you learned together?
    *Is it the same thing you are trying to learn in the current physical lifetime?
    *What is your relationship in this past life to them?

12. At this time I want you to wrap up what you are experiencing. Try and collect all the information you have received. I will count from 5 to 1 backwards, each number bringing you back to the present lifetime and full consciousness. When I reach 1 you will slowly awaken and feel refreshed and energetic. You will have full memory of everything that happened if your subconscious feels at this time it would not hurt you in any way. If your subconscious feels that you may not be ready to know certain things then those things will not be available to you at this time. However when you are ready, and with a minimum amount of pain, you will remember it all.

Lady Wolfen Mists

Ready...5 slowly awakening, 4 more awake, 3, 2, almost fully awake you can write down what you remember in your notebook upon full awakening if you like, and 1 fully and completely awake. Welcome back!

"Remembering What We once were or how we are all Connected. Come Howl with me under the powerful Moon, Our eyes see each others souls"

Notes On Class 4

Wolfen Wicca 2
Our Walk Onward To Initiation
Class #5

© Lady Wolfen Mists Jan.1990
revised 2001

Theory:
  Glossary of Common terms
  List of Goddess Names
  Intro Wards
  Wards, How to make them
  Your Sacred Sanctuary

Practical:
  Making a Ward

Circle Work:
What is your inspirational thought for the week.

***Assignment: *** **Students in your Magickal Journal:**
This week you are to draw, build or get photos and paste them of a Sacred Garden with an Altar. Show where you would place everything, and where you would place Wards for Protection. If you choose to add any other wards, Please explain where & why you placed them where you did. Also, be sure to include what they would be used for. Let your imagination soar and have fun with this! It can be as intense or as sparse as you would like. You don't have to be an artist, just "blue print" placement of things. This will be reviewed when you submit your work for Initiation ☺

"I Walk On!"

Wolfen Wicca 2
Class #5
Glossary of common Terms

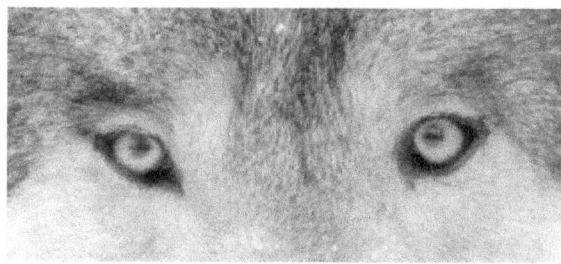

I want to make it clear that this is a compilation of peoples work and not solely mine. I am unsure of many of the authors but I found it helpful to have a glossary of the more common terms. Place it in your Book of Shadows for reference.

This list is by no means exhaustive but is very informative and helpful for those who need any clarification on words that are common to paganism. I don't agree, in full, with <u>all the definitions</u>, but it does give you a place to start from

Glossary of Commonly Used Terms

Adept   Any Serious student who has studied and accomplished degrees or levels and is believed to be highly proficient in occult systems of magick. This level is more than a beginner level but not a master yet. IE. Dedicant like level

Akashic Records: Edgar Cayce made this popular through his readings on the idea of the thought form of Akashic records. They are said Higher Astral levels. and contain data bases of personal information. They may be able to be accessed by those with many years of work, or gifted persons for the information it contains. This information is usually only revealed for positive Higher Self. Such information one can peruse by astral self or Dreamtime work, Each individual being has a section as well as such subjects as past lives, healing, Compassion levels and other magickal/spiritual practices.

Altar: (Not alter, Alter is to change something, Altar is a sacred space) A sacred place often flat like a table, on which one conducts magickal work. It is not used for anything else if possible. If used for other reasons, at the very least a special altar cloth is used to cover the surface

Glossary of common Terms page 2

Arcana: This is the Tarot deck, which is separated into 2 sections. The Major Arcana refers to (first 21 cards) or Numbered non-suit cards. The Minor Arcana is usually of 56, in some cases more depending on the deck. They contain suits of Wands, Swords, Cups & Pentacles (sometimes called the lesser Arcana)

Asperge- This is a "group of branches" of natural shrub, tree or herb, which are tied together in a ceremony, and then used to dispel negative energies from an area. Some type of Holy water is poured over the bundle and then the bundle is lightly shaken . The holy water is then dispersed by the shaking motion, and negativity is removed. One example of an Herb used as an Asperge is Hyssop

Astral Body- A non-physical etheric body. It is sometimes referred to as the Spirit/Soul. It is attached to the physical body by a "Silver Cord" usually called the etheric umbilical cord. This cord allows one's astral body to progress through the physical plane, as well as time and space with ease.

Astral Plane- This is an actual non-physical area of existence. One's astral body can reach this level when death occurs, and also during astral projection. There are many entities who dwell here. These may include; Elementals, Ghosts, Higher Spirit Guides, as well as the astral bodies living beings in the dream state. These are just a few, but you get the idea.

Astral Projection- This is often called astral travel or referred to as an Out of Body Experience (OBE). This is when the physical body separates from the astral body, and the astral part is able to travel throughout the physical world as well as other existence levels.

Aura This is the electrical field that surrounds all living being. A form of Light is created by the electromagnetic energies, which then causes a different color that individuals can be trained to see. The colors represent different meanings in the aura and these meanings can be seen and understood by trained observers.

Bi-location: In this advanced instance of Astral Travel the person has the ability to move and work on the astral realm, while also working in the physical simultaneously. However, one must have years of experience and skill to do this.

Glossary of common Terms page 3

Bind : This is stop or limit a spell (magickally) so that it will not cause harm to anyone. However, in Wolfen Wicca® we consider it unethical to bind people other than yourself. It breaks the Harm Ye None rule. But there may be times when there is no other option, and it should not be done hastily.

BURNING TIMES : This term refers to a period of persecution towards followers of the Craft as well as innocent people, during the Middle Ages and later. There is a great of argument regarding the actual of number of people who were killed, but irregardless, it was a terrible time in History. Because a majority of the people killed were women, it is often referred to as the Women's Holocaust.

Ceremonial Magick- This is a highly advanced system of magick that tries to control nature and all its power. Practitioners in this system are known to conjure spirits, either angelic or demonic by using the names of specific God(s) or archaic words of power. It requires the practitioner to utilize complicated rituals, ceremonial clothing, and special tools that are used only for a magickal purposes. The supplies for this type of Magick can be very costly. Rituals are usually very hermetic(particular) and must be done precisely as written with no room to improvise at all.

Channeling: This Technique is where a person "steps aside" to allow an entity "borrow" your body in order to speak to others either through automatic writing or verbally." Channeling is somewhat similar to what a medium does.

CHARGE OF THE GODDESS:
1. These are the words used to call the spirit of the Goddess into the High Priestess at the Esbats(full moon celebration)
2. Some feel that these words are also Goddess speaking to Her followers, or "hidden children" Generally the words of the Goddess are shared with the coven by the High Priestess.

Circle, Magick : This area is in the form of a sphere, where magical energies are present and the Wiccan rituals are practiced. The area inside the circle is considered sacred ground in which Wicca and their Deities meet. The circle is banished after each use.

Glossary of common Terms page 4

Cone of Power: This is the energy that the solitary practitioner or coven members creates/raises/generates to be sent out to the universe (by their will) for the purpose of working the intended magick.

Coven : This is a group of Witches who have organized to meet, worship and create magick together. Covens are generally (but not always) led by a High Priestess (at the very least) and a High Priest. The number of members can range from as few as 2 to 200 or more depending on the tradition being followed. Much has been written that there has to be 13 members for a coven. This is not exactly true, since it can vary greatly for each coven, depending on what the members want.

COVENSTEAD This is usually the main place for members of the coven to meet. It is often the home of the High Priestess or High Priest or even a designated meeting place. Traditionally, there was a 20 mile distance between each covenstead. In some instances, it was a 50 mile distance. This means that if there is an established covenstead in a certain area, then another coven can't move into that area, without the express permission of the High Priestess in the first covenstead. To do so is considered a serious breach of conduct. The people involved are seen as without honor. Always remember that Witch is only as good as her/his word.! In Wolfen Wicca we stick to the 50 mile distance, so if one feels this is an old and archaic rule to them I say "Merry Part "

Dedication The dedication of a Witch is the process where each person accepts the Craft as their path, and vows to study and learn all that is needed to reach the position of adept in a given tradition. In a dedication, you make a conscious choice to accept something new into your life and stand by it, no matter how difficult it may be.

Deosil This is the direction in which creative magick moves. In the northern hemisphere, this direction moves clockwise. In the southern hemisphere, this direction goes counter clockwise.

Drawing Down the Moon: : This is a popular ritual used during the Full Moon by Witches in order to draw power into themselves and join their essence with a particular deity, usually the Goddess. It is the ritual of invocation for the spirit of the Goddess to be drawn into the body of the High Priestess by the High Priest.

Glossary of common Terms page 5

Druids- These individuals were priests of the Pre-Christian Celtic beliefs. Also a type of ancient Paganism. This religion was God and Sun centered, whereas Wicca is Goddess and Moon centered There are generally 3 classifications of Druids : Prophets, Priests & Bards.

Eke Name- This refers to a witches magickal name, usually only known by members of the coven. Also can mean a witch's secret name. During the Burning Times, when persecution was running rampant, most witches had a secret name that only other coven members would know, so as to avoid persecution or death from the mainstream society.

Elder: Many Wiccan organizations often have a board of Elders who overlook the functions of the group and its variety of activities. These people have usually gotten their positions because of their experience, abilities, education, magickal expertise and sometimes counseling as well.

Exteriorization- This just another name for Astral Projection

Evocation: To call something out from within oneself. One example would be when someone calls the 4 quarters. (Not the same as invocation)

Fire Stick- This is another name for a Witches wand.

Garter- In Wicca, a garter is worn by the High Priestess, of the coven as a symbol of her rank (Witch Queen). The garter is placed above the knee and often has buckles. Each buckle denotes a grove/coven which has "hived" off the main group. This is used in both Gardnerian Wicca and also in Wolfen Wicca ® as well as other traditions

Great Rite Pays respect to the male-female polarity (God & Goddess) in the universe. It symbolizes the union of these energies on all levels of being, the physical, mental, spiritual and astral. The great rite is associated with the sacred marriage of the cncrgics. The Rite releases tremendous power levels which may be focused for magickal aims and goals. The great rite is usually performed within the magical circle and in a symbolic fashion, rather than an actual enactment. The rite is basically the High Priest plunges a ritual athame into a chalice filled with wine (or salt water) which is held by the High Priestess to show the great union.

Glossary of common Terms page 6

Handfasting- A Wiccan wedding. Generally the term is a year and a day or as the love shall last. These ceremonies are done on a waxing moon by a High Priestess, couples traditionally exchange rings inscribed with runes, a chalice and a dagger

Handparting- This is sometimes referred to as the "going of ways" It is actually quite similar to a divorce, it dissolves the handfasting completely. Most couples traditionally remain (or try to) friends.

Hoo Doo- This lively Folk Magick, mixes the European religious beliefs thoughts/techniques with VooDoo rituals. Centers mainly on actual techniques/rituals.

Imp- The archaic term for a witches familiar. This is not the cute friendly type more like a little demon or similar unpleasant little creature.

Initiation: An experience that so changes the individual in that their concept of reality as they know it has been transformed. Important note: a dedication ceremony should not be confused with the rite of initiation. This is usually where a practitioner is accepted into a group that follows a specific tradition. The person is now granted the rank they have earned through hard work. Generally it is accepted that the process to achieve the traditional 1st degree ranking is study for 1 year and a day..

Invocation : The ritual "calling-in" of an entity (or energies) higher than humans, for the purpose of communication with the one who called. This can be done through a medium or by visible manifestation. For more information see the Drawing Down the Moon ritual.

Kabalah- Also goes by name like Cabbala, Qabbalah. A highly advanced, in depth system of magick, that originates with the Hebrew Scriptures. Here the followers believe in the worship of one main God/Deity that goes by 72 different names, each name radiates powerful energy. Cabalists believe there are actually 4 separate planes of being that create up the Universe.

Karma: The universes checks and balances your actions. Everything you do can result in Karma coming after you. Unfortunately the act of doing Good Karma can not get rid up bad karma as all debts must be paid, but the universe never expects you to pay anything you are not spiritually ready to do. This is very brief but you get the picture. There's more to it than the brief explanation given here. In Sanskrit,

Glossary of common Terms page 7

it means "action." Follow the law of cause and effect.

Left Hand Path- This is the practice of Black Magick, Sorcery, or other negativity based energy systems.

Machi- (Araucanian Indians) These are female Shamans who do the healing.

Magician- A practices Ceremonial or ritual magick with no particular religious beliefs. This per is skilled in magickal techniques, without worship aspects involved.

Magick- This is the traditional spelling with a "K," and is used to tell the difference between Theater Magic and Mystical Magick. The practice of Magick is the orchestration of natural energies to create the events/results that the practitioner wishes.

Mara- According to folk legends, this is a female elf friendly towards humans.

Old Religion: Another name for the Craft.

Oracle- A consecrated site to a particular Deity where a person would reveal answers to questions.

Pagan- Latin (Paganus) means "Country Dweller" Any religious believer or sect that is not Christian, (IE Wiccan, Jew, Hindu, etc.) Often used by Christian Church officials in a non flattering/derogatory way.

PATHWORKING: This is a Wiccan Journey through the astral realm. It is narrated and occurs often in groups. There usually .is a set destination that all arrive at a certain place.

Practical Magick- A system of simple Folk Magick that uses common tools with in the practice, (IE. besom=broom, athema=kitchen knifes) This is usually thought of as the common peoples system of magick. It is based on balance, Harmony, Nature, and the never ending cycle of birth, life, death, & rebirth. Supplies for this system of magick are traditionally multi-purpose and can be found in inexpensive places, like thrift stores, yard sales, and so on. This system is very open to personal spontaneity and interpretation.

Quarters: The four directions (North, East, South, and West) quarters of a magickal circle or other ritual area.

Glossary of common Terms page 8

Reincarnation: The belief of rebirth after death into a new life, and that one has lived many lifetimes in different places and realms.

Santeria- Spanish (Santo) translates to "the worship of Saints" This system of magick joins both African Magick and Catholic worship traditions. It is much like Voodoo. It is based in nature, various deities are worshipped. Each god or goddess requires certain sacrifices (sometimes corn, food or blood. etc.) when one wishes the deity to grant them a favor or boon.

Transmigration- A term used for the soul reincarnating into a different species of physical body, can be human or non-human. Often thought that the next body one receives, reflects how you did in a past life. If you lead a good life, them you move up to the next higher level/body. The opposite is true for a negatively lead past/present life.

True Magick- This is magick that is done according to the Wiccan Rede (and harm ye none.). Its usually helpful, positive & healing in nature. Sometimes called White Magick

Warlock- A VERY derogatory term for **Male Witch**. Thought to come from the old English word "WAERLOGA" meaning "Oath Breaker" Male Wiccans are Witches period.

Wiccaning- A special rite preformed for a baby, similar to a baptism.. The baby is given the (magickal) name by the parents. Then is dedicated to the Bright Lady and Lord. The God/dess are asked to bless the child, to instill powers and to protect the child all the days of its life. Also called Paganing

Widdershins: The counter clock wise movement (usually inside the circle or in spellcasting) that is The unraveling of Power as opposed to Deosil which is the building of power in a clock wise direction.

Witchling- Another name for a Witch's child.

Wizard- Taken from Old English word "WIS" meaning "wise". Sometimes male witches were referred to as "wizards."

Wortcunning- Pertains to the knowledge & practice of herbs. Knowing medical & magickal properties. The act of harvesting herbs and drying in their natural form

Glossary of common Terms page 9

Zoanthropy- "Shape Shifting" Belief that a person can change shape. They become an animal, taking the animals characteristics & traits on. Also known as Otherkin

Zoomorphism- The act/ability of changing shape from human to animal or animal to human, this is done by use of magick, amulets, talismans, spells, hexes, or incantations. The most well known form of this is lycanthropy, changing from human form to wolf form.

Lady Wolfen Mists

Wolfen Wicca 2
Class #5
List of Goddess names & Attributes

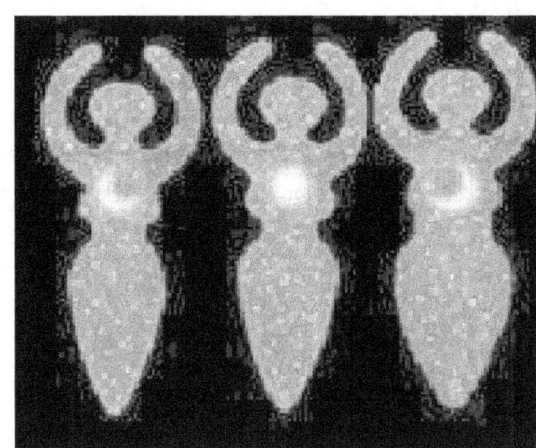

There are times we wish to call upon a specific Goddess aspect in a specific pantheon. I have attempted here to give you a listing of the more popular ones often used. It is by no means exhaustive but will give you a foundation to start with and a direction to go from if you are looking for more.

Anaitis	Goddess of Fertility (Persian)
Ananna	Goddess of Plenty and Fertility, Mother aspect of Goddess (Celtic)
Aphrodite	Goddess of Love & Beauty (Greek)
Artemis	Goddess of Moon, Hunting & Wild Beasts (Greek) See Diana (Roman)
Arianrhod	Goddess of the Sky, Stars & Reincarnation Mother Aspect of Goddess Her time is at the Full Moon (Celtic, Wales)
Astarte	Goddess of Love & Fertility (Phoenician)
Athena	Goddess of Wisdom & the Arts, Warrior aspect of the Goddess (Greek) See Minerva (Roman)
Bast	Goddess of Fertility, Hearth Also called "Lady Of Light", Denotes gentle healing power of the Sun (Egyptian)

Class #5
List of Goddess names & Attributes
Page 2

Bona Dea	Goddess of Purity, Chastity and Fertility Her worship was (is) restricted to women only May 1st is her festival day (Roman)
Branwen	Goddess of Love and Beauty Called "Lady of the Lake" (Wales, Manx)
Brighid	Goddess of Hearth, Fire, Healing, Physicians, Agriculture, Inspiration, Learning, Divination, Smith-crafting, Witchcraft, Occult Knowledge, All Feminine Arts, Etc. Triple Goddess Aspects, She is one of the few Goddess that was turned into a Saint when Christianity took over.
Ceres	Goddess of Harvest & fertility (Roman) See Demeter (Greek)
Cerridwen	Goddess of the Moon, Fertility, Death, Regeneration, Inspiration, poetry, Spell Work, Herbal Magick & Healing Sciences, etc. Main Triple Goddess (Celtic)
Chicomecoatl	Goddess of Nourishment & Good Crops (Aztec)
Demeter	Goddess of Husbandry, Harvest & Fertility (Greek)
Diana	Goddess of the Hunt Lunar Goddess Virgin aspect of Goddess (Roman)
Eostre	Goddess of Springtime, Abundance, Fertility (Saxon)
Ereshkigal	Goddess and Queen of the Underworld, Horned Goddess (Sumerian)
Fortuna	Goddess of Luck, Good Fortune, Chance & Happiness (Roman)
Freya	Goddess of Fertility, Love, & Beauty (Scandinavian)
Frigga	Goddess of Marriage Mother Goddess (Scandinavian)
Gula	Goddess of Healing & Creativity (Babylonian)

Class #5
List of Goddess names & Attributes
Page 3

Hathor	Goddess of Infants, Music, Love, Beauty & the Heavens (Egyptian)
Hecate	Goddess of Witchcraft, Wisdom, Justice, Discipline. Patroness of all Witches Crone aspect of the Goddess (Roman)
Hera	Goddess of Marriage & Birth (Greek)
Isis	Goddess of Motherhood, Magick Her spells bring the dead back to life Queen of Death (Egyptian)
Kali	Goddess of Death (Hindu)
Kupala	Goddess of Life, Sex & Vitality (Slavic)
Laka	Goddess of Rain & Rainstorms (Hawaiian)
Lakshimi	Goddess of the Lotus (Hindu)
Lucina	Goddess of Childbirth (Roman)
Maat	Goddess of Law & Justice (Egyptian)
Mahuika	Goddess of Fire, Earthquakes & Underworld (Hawaiian)
MaMa Cocha	Goddess of Sea & Fishermen (Peru)
Mania	Goddess of the Dead (Roman)
Morrigan aka Morrigan, Morgan	Goddess of War, Death, Fate, Revenge, Prophecy, Magick & the Night Triple Goddess She is said to be a shape shifter her favorite shapes are the Crow & the Raven (Celtic)
Mut aka Nuit	Goddess in the Cosmic Void from which all things come. She is associated with the night sky (Egyptian)
Nemesis	Goddess of Vengeance & Anger (Greek)

Class #5
List of Goddess names & Attributes
Page 4

Net	Goddess of the hunt could be seen as a aspect of Mut (Egyptian)
Nike	Goddess of Victory (Greek)
Nuit	Goddess of Sky Mother Goddess (Egyptian)
Nyx	Goddess of the Night & Darkness (Greek)
P'an Chin Lien	Goddess of Fornication & Prostitutes (Chinese)
Parvati	Goddess of Mountains, Sprites, Elves & rules Nature Spirits (Hindu)
Rhiannon	Goddess of Horses, Birds, all most anything quick & swift, Enchantments, Music & Underworld (Celtic)
Scath	Dark Goddess of the Underworld. Her reign covers Martial Arts, Magick, Healing, Prophecy Aids Blacksmiths (Celtic)
Selene	Goddess of the Moon in waxing aspect (Greek)
Sekhmet	Sister of Bast. She is the Dark aspect of the sun, she shows the power of the Sun to destroy. The sun in desert like conditions. She also has great Healing energies, and protective spirit to those Loyal to Her (Egyptian)
Tlazolteotl	Goddess of Love, Fertility, Earth Also called Mother of all Gods (Aztec)
Venus	Goddess of Love & Beauty & Good Fortune (Roman)
Vesta	Goddess of Home & Hearth (Roman)

Wolfen Wicca 2
Class #5
Wards: Introduction

© Lady Wolfen Mists

Wards are types of items that are made, infused or programmed for one specific purpose or reason. Wards, unlike Talismans or Amulets, wear out or power down and need to be replaced at specific intervals. The reason for this is that wards use immense amounts of energies and that energy level needs to be restored so that the ward can continue to function at optimum levels. Traditionally, we see that wards have been used for protection, but it can also be for other things. Wards are usually tangible in nature, something you can touch on the physical level, but (traditionally) represent an item on the Astral level. Got that? Easy isn't it.

For those of you who didn't get it from that explanation, let me give you an example. Lets suppose that you want a Astral Dragon to protect you from a psychic Vampire. The Vampire seems to attack you no matter how much you call up the White Light, especially when you sleep. You plan to continue to use the White light but would like some extra help. You decide that an Astral Level Dragon would work well for you, but you are unsure how to call one up. What on the physical level would draw Dragon to you? Well its said that raw Amethyst (especially clusters) are used by dragons to feed on, the positive "Higher Self" energies help to energize them and resonate with their vibrational level. So on the physical level you could get an Amethyst cluster and turn it into a ward, drawing the dragon to you. The cluster would be your connection to the ward and would show you when it needed to be replace/repowered. In this case, you would see the clusters color changing, it would also loss its clarity. You would begin to see "dirt" inside the crystals. Most importantly it "feels" sticky and dirty and can"t be cleaned no matter how hard you try.

What do you do, you can feel the ward weakening. You need to replace the Amethyst as it has been "used up" and use one of the following methods to make it a ward, just like the other one. The old Amethyst will need to be buried or placed under leafs or grass, you must leave it behind and not return to it. The stone is returned to the Source (the Mother) and She will take it within herself and slowly "heal" it.

Wards: Introduction page 2

It should be noted here that the Amethyst need not be the most expensive one you can find, it just needs to feel harmonious in its vibrational field. By "feeding" your Dragon often you can be assured that it will act as your guardian on the Astral level for many years to come.

Wolfen Wicca 2
Class #5
Methods of Making Wards

© Lady Wolfen Mists

What Is A Ward?

Lets talk about wards. They are magickal creations that you put energies into for a specific purpose. Usually people make protective wards to keep away negative energies, and place them around their homes, so they don't have to keep remembering to put up protective shields. Windows and doorways are good places to put wards. However I don't want you to think the only kind of ward is a protective one, a ward can encompass anything you like it to, from a ward for abundance, to one to draw your familiar home. You name it, it can be a ward. Wards are usually made of natural materials (but this is up to you. It is said natural is better because they cant be broken as easily. Think of wards much like a security system, they are set by you, empowered by you and controlled by you. Yet there are those who can break weak wards and enter your security system, the only way to stop this is to pratice making wards so that they become stronger and more efficient. This is where you begin to learn to imbue items with your magickal energies, they may be weak at first but as you grow in knowledge, power and wisdom so will your ability to make these wonderful items.

Steps To Making Them

The following information gives you the step by step procedure for making wards of your own. I don't recommend one over the other as I have tried them all and got excellent results, some people however prefer to use the method that best resonates to their elemental self's. For example if you were a "Fire/Earth" based person you may prefer, and get better results, using the Flame method for constructing your wards. Now with that in mind lets begin!

Class #5
Methods of Making Wards
Page 2

FLAME METHOD

You will be using a crystal or stone here but any object will work. The example given here is a Protection incantation, but remember, the situation can be created to fit your needs. These are just examples

1. Take the crystal or stone and cleanse it completely in salt water, allow it to soak. This removes any negativity vibrations that the item may contain and readies it for your programming.

2. While cleansing the item, light a red candle. Be sure to anoint the candle with a general positive oil. I like Goddess oil or Celtic Holy/Healing oil, but you may use any, just be sure its a general positive oil

3. Next take your item out of the water and dry it off.

4. Next take the item, in this case a stone, and hold it in both hands. With it setting between your thumbs focus your attention on the item. While you are holding the item visualize the person you wish to protect. "SEE" everything about them. Now pull the White Light into yourself, through the crown chakra and allow it to build within you. Once it has built to a significant amount, begin
to shape and focus these energies. Focus and "move" these energies to the Third eye and Heart Chakra. Project theses energies from both of these chakra points into the item (stone). See the item accepting this energy and setting up a "mini" generator inside the item, itself. This allows the energies that you send, to regenerate that clean clear cleansing light that will protect the person you give or make this ward for.

5. It is at this point. Where the energies are sent into the item that <u>Concentration</u> is key. Without concentration & visualization you are wasting your time.

6. Once you have completed the steps above your ready to move on to "setting & sealing" the energies. Take the item (stone) and pass it through the flame of the red candle three (3) times. You MUST pass the item in a **<u>right to left</u>** direction a total of three (3) times.

Class #5
Methods of Making Wards
Page 3

7. Say the following, or something like it, when passing the item through the flame.

**"Do not let Negativity touch (name), May this ward keep them safe and protected.
Do not let negativity exist around them. As I have willed it,
So Mote It Be!"**

8. You are finished, put your ward away or give it to the person for which it is intended. Put out the candle, and clean up.

WATER/WAX METHOD
This method will be using a nut or shell, but you can use anything. The situation used here is another Protection and a Success & Wealth incantation but you can vary the situation to fit your needs.

1. Take the nut or shell and cleanse it completely in salt water, allow it to soak. This removes any negative vibrations that the item may contain and readies it for your programming.

2. Next take your item out of the water and dry it off.

3. Next choose the candle you will be using, anoint with oil and light. These examples use a White candle for Protection, and a Orange candle for Attraction. Be sure to anoint the candle with a general positive natured oil for the protection one. I like Goddess oil or Celtic Holy/Healing oil, or even Protection oil, but when all else fails us Moon Water Oil. You may use any you like, this is just to give you ideas, be sure its a general positive oil. For the wealth and success one you can use an oil for Wealth & Success, or even one for Abundance. Again the choice is up to you.

4. Pour a small bowl of Holy Water. We use what we call Metaphysically Correct Holy Water, which is different than Church Holy Water. This type of water was created on a Full moon with just the right cleansing energies and ingredients. The reason it is "Holy" is that it is created on a sacred night (full moon) usually within a sacred place (circle) and infused with White Light and positive energy and cleansing ingredients, thus "Metaphysically Correct Holy Water" If you don't have Holy Water you can use rose water as a substitute, but I like the Holy water better.

5. Now use some of the anointing oil on the item you are making a ward from. Just a drop or two should do it. While you are holding the item visualize the person you

Wolfen Wicca 2; Our Walk Onward To Initiation

Class #5
Methods of Making Wards
Page 4

wish to protect or the amount of Wealth/Success you wish to acquire. "SEE" everything about them/it. Now pull down the White Light and let it flow into yourself. Start at the crown chakra and allow it to build within you. Once it has built to a significant amount, begin to shape and focus these energies. Focus and "move" these energies to the Third eye and Heart Chakra. Project theses energies from both of these chakra points into the item being used. See the item filling/accepting the energy and setting up a "mini" generator inside itself.

6. To "set" these energies that you have infused into the item, you will now place the item in the bowl of Holy Water. Allow it to be submerged for at least 13 heartbeats, more if you like.

7. Place the bowl in front of the candle (that has been burning) and say the following: remember that this varies with whatever you intend the ward to do. I have include words for Protection and Wealth & Success but these are just guides, allow yourself to be creative!

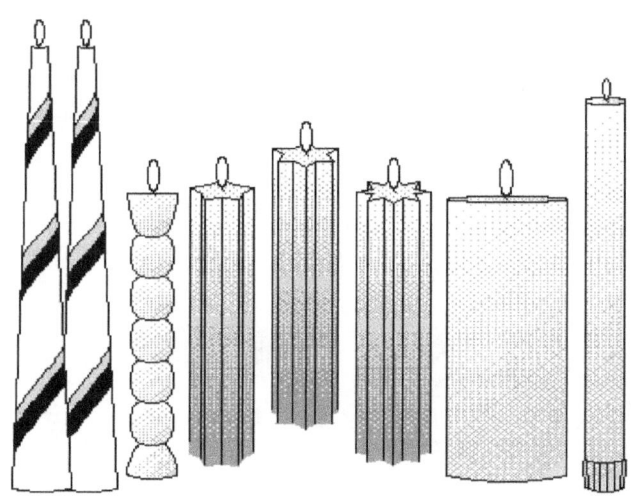

WHITE CANDLE for Protection

> "In this item I have infused the protection given by the Lady Of Light.
> As Long as it is carried it will protect and aid, <u>name.</u>
> This ward will keep Her/Him safe.
> No type of negativity may pierce this shield and touch them,
> no harm may be sent or come to them.
> As I have willed it, So Mote It Be! "

Class #5
Methods of Making Wards
Page 5

ORANGE CANDLE for Wealth & Success

"In this item I have infused the power to attract on positive and abundant energies. Energies of Success & Wealth.
May <u>name,</u> find only prosperity and success in His/Her days.
As long as this ward is used or carried, may my wished be made true.
As I have willed it, So Mote It Be!"

8. You are finished, put your ward away or give it to the person for which it is intended. Put out the candle, and clean up.

Wolfen Wicca 201
Class #5
Your Sacred Sanctuary

© Lady Wolfen Mists 1992

A luscious green garden, generating tons of psychic energies. Those energies reaching out to you, drawing you to it. It becomes your magickal impenetrable fortress, keeping all unwanted energies at bay and enfolding you in healing energizing sensations. It's a place for worship, relaxation, meditation, and study. It becomes your cocoon where you escape from the abuses of the day, its healing energies soothing you and touching your soul. It has been built to your specifications, a holy, sacred, consecrated place and it's all yours.

The following are steps used to build your sacred sanctuary, and to make it like the one described above;

Step 1   <u>Getting ready to build your Sacred Sanctuary</u>
-Find a special place where you can relax and release the stress of the day.

-It should be an actual physical place, that may draw you to it, or one that you can develop in your mind's eye, the way your imagination guides you to do.

-Once you find your place you're ready to move one to

Step 2   <u>Cleansing the area: on the Physical plane</u>
-Pick up any litter, trim grass or hedges, tidy area.

Class #5
Your Sacred Sanctuary
Page 2

- Sprinkle with Metaphysical correct Holy Water, and sea salt the night before a full moon.

Step 3 Cleansing the area on the Emotional plane

- Place a programmed crystal (programmed for protection and the enhancement of positive energies), in the center of the Sanctuary

- The crystal should be placed in a hole, far enough into the Earth that the dirt covers the entire stone, with the point up. *(See Diagram A below)*

- Go to each quarter (N, E, S, N) and ask the elements to come and cleanse, protect and make fertile their particular corner.

- Dig a small hole at the edge of each of the four section's boarders, and place a piece of obsidian in each hole.

- Replace the dirt being sure to cover three stones completely. (*See Diagram A below*)

- Do this on the same night as the cleansing of the physical plane, the night before the full moon.

Step 4 Cleansing the area on the Spiritual Plane

- On the evening of the FULL moon cast your circle out in the chosen area.

- Use your wand and purify the area, drawing the white light down thru you and out the crystal wand.

- Allow your "visualization" of what this place should be, what you want it to become, to flow out the wand with the White light.

Empowering the tools needed to build

Visualize the items you will need to build your sanctuary the way you like. Rock, wood, herbs, flowers, water, grass, fountains, bird feeders and so on. "See" these items in your mind's eye and what you will build with each one. Create the sanctuary in your mind, the way you would want it to look! Now Visualize all the beings you would wish to dwell herein: Animals, Elementals, Fairies, Devas, Your personal spirit guides or Power animals. Be sure to "feed" you beings often. For

Class #5
Your Sacred Sanctuary
Page 3

example, lets say you call Devas to live at your place. You would want to make sure there were plenty of flowering plants for them to hide, play and live in. Water for them to drink and bath in. Or perhaps you call a Dragon to come live in your Sanctuary, which could be used to represent the element of fire.

Anyway, you would want to "feed" your Dragon Crystal, Amethyst or Citrine clusters. You would place these clusters throughout the Sanctuary, in different sections, around the Dragons Lair. This sets up the needed energy lines and forces that feed or retain your dragon's presence in your special place. Just be sure that you represent all four (4) of the elements in some way, within the appropriate area of your garden.

Naming and it's power

Once you have begun the actual physical placement and construction of your Sanctuary be sure to name it. Naming something is a very powerful practice in itself. To know and call the name of an object or person gives you great power over shaping it, you not only "call" it in to being, but you have the power to shape it by its name. The name of your Sanctuary should be one that represents the very essence of the total sum of your magickal belief system. It should be one that inspires and motivates, one that inflames the imagination and kindles the soul. A name that speaks of Glory, Esteem and Honor to the Creator and Creatress of all things. Pretty tall order isn't it? That's why you should put a lot of time and consideration into the name you chose and the energies you, in the end, call into existence.

Once you have decided upon a name, this can be done at any moon phase, go outside to the middle of the Sanctuary where the crystal is buried. Taking up your wand once more, facing the North with the wand in your dominate hand, say something like the following;

> "Hear me, Master of the Solar Light,
> May your wild beings find safety and security here,
> in this space I have created.
>
> Hear me Most Splendid Enchantress of the Moon lit night
> May your never ending beauty grace these walks,
> these flowers, this creation built in your honor.
>
> For I, (Your magickal name),
> who have created this sanctuary to exalt the beauty and
> nurturance of the Great Earth Mother.
> To the wild fierceness and passions of the Great Horned One,
> do consecrate this sanctuary to their positive and unconditional

Class #5
Your Sacred Sanctuary
Page 4

> loving light, making it HOLY ground.
> I do hereby name it   (name of sanctuary).
> So Mote It Be!"

Now turn to face the South and invoke a pentagram connecting all the power girds and every energy line you have created within your sanctuary! (*See Diagram B*)

One last note if you want to place an altar within your sanctuary, the place that is in the center, over the crystal is <u>perfect</u> for this! The altar would benefit from all the energies that are now connected and flow around and through that spot, and think of the additional power it might lend to any magickal work you might preform there.

Completed and ready to use

With all the above finished you have successfully completed the setup and making of your perfect place. But you will most likely find it is never truly done. You will continue adding and rearranging for many years to come. It may be something as simple as a sundial or as complicated as an herb garden designed to grow and bloom in a star pattern. But no matter what you continue to add or replace, just remember it is your fortress! It is your magickal space on this, often times abusive, physical plane. Be sure to take time to arrange and prepare it, allowing it the conditions needed for it to operate at it's optimize level. But above all this let it reflect the magick within your soul!

Wolfen Wicca 2
Class #5
Your Sacred Sanctuary
Diagrams A & B

© Lady Wolfen Mists

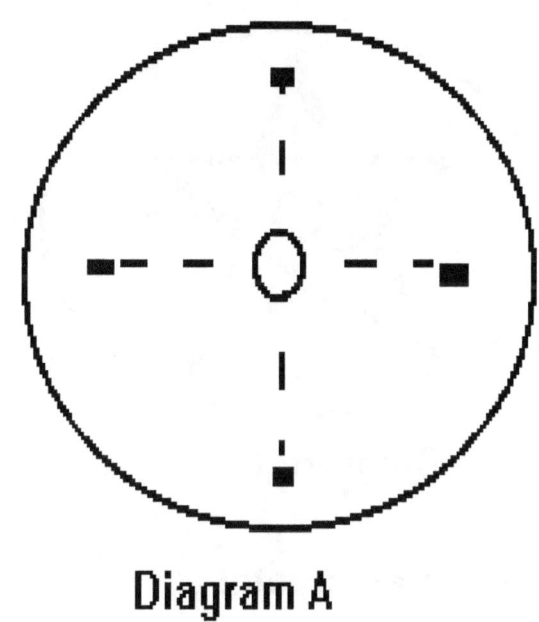

Diagram A

○ denotes crystal
— denotes enery lines
■ denotes obsidian

Lady Wolfen Mists

Wolfen Wicca 2
Class #5
Diagrams A & B Page 2

© Lady Wolfen Mists

Diagram B

○ denotes crystal
---- denotes enery lines
■ denotes obsidian
━ denotes wand energy lines from invoking pentagram

Wolfen Wicca 2
Class # 5
Practical: Using A Nut to Make a Ward

©Lady Wolfen Mists

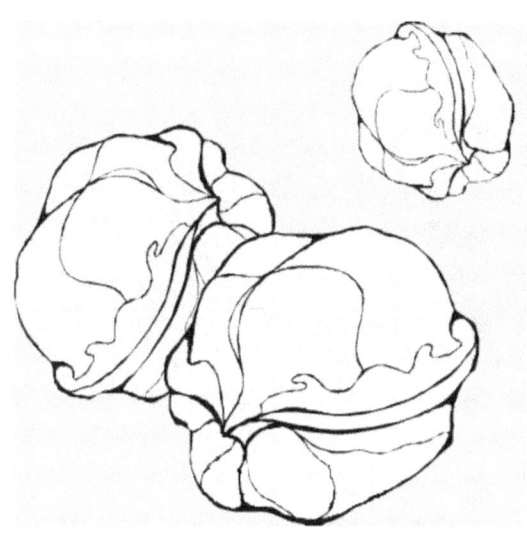

Instructions to the Practical Section

Use the prior instructions given, on making wards, and choose a method you like best. Then using a Nut (like a walnut) make a ward. Follow the instructions given in the theory section and you should have no problems at all! Bright Blessings to you.

Notes on Ward Making

Notes On Class 5

Lady Wolfen Mists

Wolfen Wicca 2
Our Walk Onward To Initiation
Class #6

© Lady Wolfen Mists Jan.1990
revised 2001

Theory:
   Types of wolves in the magickal sense
   Familiars in General
   Familiar Spell
   Familiar Oil Recipe
   Color Chart to refer to
   Magickal Sand Painting
   Symbols

Practical:
   Magickal Sand Mosaic

Circle Work:
   What is your inspirational thought for the week.

***Assignment: *** **Students in your Magickal Journal:**
   Please create your own familiar Spell. You can make it Dramatic or "Down to Earth", Complicated or Simple. But be sure to use all the steps given to you in the previous <u>Components of A Spell</u> class (see class #2). Just let it be something you are comfortable with, allow your personality to shine! There is no failure here its just putting into practice what you have been learning. This will be reviewed when you submit your work for Initiation ☺

"I Walk On!

Wolfen Wicca 2
Class #6
Types of Inner Wolves you can call on for help

© Lady Wolfen Mists Jan 22, 2015

      Each one of us walks with an inner wolf, it acts to guide us in any current situation that may arise. Wolves often denote that place inside us that bespeaks of freedom and the power to live life to its fullest. Our lives change and develop as we walk our sacred paths, and the faces/facets of that wolf may change as well. Always there to assist us in whatever position we may find ourselves. The wolf is a loyal pack member and as such exhibits many many different faces but each one is still wolf and still an important part of that overall wolf, just as we may have many roles in life and titles all together it makes the whole of us. Here are **a few** of the more often used and seen wolves, there are many others.

Class #6
Types of Inner Wolves you can call on for help
Page 2

The Strong powerful large wolf Many people wonder what it means when a strong powerful large wolf appears in their lives, in dreams, in songs. You keep seeing this powerful wolf all about you, pictures, advertizements and so on. It is there and many wonder what the universe is trying to say. Well when this powerful wolf manifests its presence it could be telling you to live your life with more freedom, not so structured patterns. Loosen us and feel the freedom and intensity as well as passion in your everyday undertakings.

The Sleek a bit bedraggle wolf, Perhaps you are seeing a sleek a bit bedraggle wolf, slightly underfed but with that hungry look in its eyes. Eyes that seem to bore though you to your very soul. This is the facet that is not easily domesticated, always a bit of wildness remains that can never be tamed. Their appearance most commonly means that there is a need to look at what supports your genuine self. This would also include what it takes to find and be the true manifestation of who you are in your Higher Self. This facet, as scraggly as it may be is a constant reminder that you and you alone are the one responsible for keeping your spirit alive through the freedom in your soul, and trusting your instincts to find the path that you need to walk to be true to who you are!

The Black/silver snarling wolf who represents the menace of being threatened. This threat can be from the outside of you, your environment, or threats to yourself through your own actions, like diminishing and trapping who you truly are inside, locking up the true you to fit in as society expects. This wolf will help you deal with people, events, situations, even traumatic situations that you felt you have little control over. It will help you learn to deal with that overbearing boss in a positive, yet assertive manner that will prove your worth on the job. That you are very efficient in that position and more than competent for the job. Other situations can be rewritten as well, even those traumatic events that seem to have taken part of your soul. This wolf returns what is yours, it reminds you of responsibly not just to the event that occurred but to yourself, so you are NOT taking on the responsibility that was not yours or the guilt that did not belong to you. It helps remove the fear of what you went through or saw or you may have a part of. It rewrites the event in truth and not in the "colored" film that you see in your minds eye. This wolf does not allow for threats of any kind to control you in any manner and speaks its truth loudly and in a healing manner, bringing you back to who you were meant to be in your total healthy self.

Wolfen Wicca 2; Our Walk Onward To Initiation

Class #6
Types of Inner Wolves you can call on for help
Page 3

The Parent wolf Mother/Father Teacher Large Iridescent White fluffy Wolf with eyes that seem to observe and catch everything. This is the wolf facet that Holds the "family" close, it acts as a teacher and it shows you unconditional love. Maybe you always felt left out of things, you lacked the love you needed, this facet show you in a positive healthy way how to met those needs. When you need to reach inside for a loving hug or understanding this wolf teaches you how important learning self acceptance and self love is. This wolf also teaches you how very important teaching is and how you are a vessel of these lighted energies, how you must learn to pass those ideas, thoughts, feelings, rituals down to the up coming new cubs and elders.

The Pup wolf This is the wolf facet that reminds you how important it is to play and have fun, no matter your age. It points out the things that are truly important in life, not the made up necessities that society tells us we MUST have. It helps to heal childhood & adulthood wounds and deep scars on levels that will cause you the least amount of pain to remember, while giving you healing suggestions that are perfect for your individual case. It rejuvenates the soul and spirit and it is just plain fun. It renews the wish to learn (so great for students) and allows you to see obstacles from a fresh perspective. This wonderful pup helps take us from the tedium of daily life and infuses us to play and have fun once more.

The Sexy wolf - Again a wolf of powerful personal instincts that shows you the people in your life manipulating you. There is a strong sexual energy here that many could feel is aggressive or even domineering, this could be on the emotional, physical or spiritual level and one would do well to listen and keep these beings energies in check so as to not become a puppet to another. This wolf is often called to even out relationships in which you feel used or controlled in, that you are fearful of. Although this is sexual in nature it does over lap into daily interaction with others who try this same tactics to keep you beaten down

Class #6
Types of Inner Wolves you can call on for help
Page 4

The Pack wolf Is an amazing wolf who warns us that our boundaries have been over stepped. This is the wolf that protects you from painful memories you are not ready to deal with or situations where you may feel you have "over shared" and exposed yourself to much. It is this pack wolf that you call for positive reinforcement of what you need on all levels, emotional, physical and spiritual. This wolf will walk beside you and remind you you are not alone and you have the strength and love of your entire pack at your beck and call. It will lift you up so you do not walk alone, reminding you of your "family" and protecting you from others who may exhibit negative behavior to, about and around you. This wolf is a strong competitor on your behalf and does it all with little to no violence. Just being with this wolf sets you apart and above by its energies.

Now admittedly these are just a few of the more common wolves you can call upon for help or direction, or even notice them in your life, there are many others. So if you are in need or are seeing a wolf not listed here follow your instincts and let it speak with you. Also remember that wolves are teachers and guides and help with personal instincts / situations. They would never become physically violent nor ask you to do so, they are much like spirit guides and have only your Higher self in mind., violence isn't an action of the Higher Self.

"Wise, Powerful, loving, disciplinarian, sexy, Mysterious, Majestic Wolf , A main Part of all of use that walk the Wolfen Wicca Path"

Lady Wolfen Mists

Wolfen Wicca 2
Class #6
Familiars In General

© Lady Wolfen Mists Jan.1989
revised 2001

      Familiars, by definition, are attendant spirits that take the form of various animals. These animals work with Witches as helpers and companions. Folklore from the middle ages, tells us that Black cats (a favorite familiar of witches) was said to house the spirit of other Witches who had crossed over and were waiting to reincarnate. Some people still say this and claim that when a cat looks at you it is with the eyes of another witch, filing information away to be used in the next lifetime. Interesting thoughts.......

      Familiars are said to be able to communicate on a psychic/telepathic level with their Masters, relating information from the many planes and dimensions that surround us. Some practitioners are said to have a unique talent that enables them to "Animal Speak". Meaning they can speak and understand the language of animals. Others develop a talent somewhat like this, over time and with the help of the familiar. Familiars connect with the natural powers of creation found in everyday life. This connection related/shown to us, makes us more aware of the power of the "wild", and helps us to reconnect to that power. Animals are usually more sensitive to what's going on around them, on the astral/physical planes. This helps the practitioners to become more sensitive to these surrounding energies also, and encourages us to be more confident in our own intuition. A example of this is to take note of how your familiar reacts to friends, strangers and even places. It is usually a good clue on the vibrations surrounding the people or place. If your pet tries to escape the area or from being around specific people, you should probably take a second look and not stay around them/it either.

Class #6
Familiars In General
Page 2

    Since these animals, and most animals in general, are more sensitivity to what's going on around them they play and important part in the workings of a Witch. But the choosing of a Familiar should not be done flippantly. Its a commitment that should take long consideration. Along with the many ethical issues that can come into play here, you need to consider if you can provide food, water, shelter and Love for this animal for the rest of its life. In return it will work for you and be your inseparable companion. You must also realize that upon making an animal your familiar you tie a bond between the two of you for the <u>rest of both your lives</u>. It is a great responsibility, but contains many rewards. One must always remember to keep all works positive in nature and abide by the Three Fold Law, even when asking/instructing a familiar to help.

    The familiar can be trained on the physical level to relate information to its companion (master). It can let you see what was done, hear what was said, and also if they completed that task you sent them to do. Historically this was called, "Doing Your Masters Bidding." It is here that one needs to always consider the ethical repercussions of any task one might set the familiar out to do. The familiar becomes your additional eyes, ears, and hands. Their senses can become one with yours, just as yours can become one with them, if the lines of communication are kept open. Also one MUST give and have <u>respect</u> in this relationship. Your respect for them should be as another evolving soul, who has intelligence and feelings, just as you do. When a familiar is treated well it will choose to be your working/loving companion for many years to come. It should also be noted here that a familiar has a choice in becoming "yours" or not. It, like all other living beings in the universe, has free will. They, like us, are on a spiritual quest too. So as you can see, familiars can become a very valuable tool in your arsenal for the light.

Lady Wolfen Mists

Wolfen Wicca 2
Class #6
Familiar Spell

© Lady Wolfen Mists Jan.1989
revised 2001

Color equivalency list for eyes of animal Stones used to represent those colors

Brown eyes	Gold colored stone
Blue eyes	Blue stone
Green eyes	Green stone
Hazel eyes	Aqua stone
Lavender eyes	Lt. Purple stone

Color List & Reasons for use of specific cords

Purple = for Higher Self
Blue = Healing & Communication
Red = For fiery passionate Energies

Full altar setup and circle cast to do this spell. If solitary you do all the parts

ITEMS NEEDED:

Matches & Burner

Red cat Image candle

Color stones for eyes

Colored cords X 3

Familiar Oil

Wolfen Wicca 2; Our Walk Onward To Initiation

Moon Water Oil

Your own nail & hair clippings

Friendship Incense (Vanilla works well or sandalwood)

Stuffed Animal: one chosen to represent physical presence of your familiar

This spell is best done on a waxing or full moon. Circle is cast as usual with altar set up as usual. Place red cat image candle on the side tray in front or beside altar.

Highest Ranking Oracle or High Priestess

> "Tonight we gather to seal the psychic bond between our pets and ourselves. Let all who wish to create this bond sit in a circle."

All sit down in a circle, facing each other. The ranking Oracle hands out the red candles. Holding the Familiar oil in one hand, and saying the following:

Oracle/High Priestess:

> "This oil, made to bring forth the wisdom and the wildness of an animal, yet granting control and discipline, shall be used to dress your candle.
>
> "Visualize your animal and the qualities that animal has. I Infuse those same qualities into this candle. Include those qualities you wish this animal to gain. Grant it wisdom, understanding, and communication with you. Dress it now!"

(Wait for all to dress candles)

Oracle/High Priestess:

> "Next bring forth those parts of your animal that you have brought. Place these items on the right side of your candle, seal with the wax from the white taper if need be. When you have done this take nail clippings and hair from yourself. Place these on the left side of your red

candle, seal it with wax if needed.

Now choose a clear (rhinestone or natural stone can be used) stone for the right eye. Next, choose one stone, of the appropriate color to match your eye color. Place it in the left eye of the candle."

"Once this is done Braid the three (3) cords you have. "See" the qualities you infused when you dressed the candle. "Feel" the bond being made. Link by link, an unbreakable psychic chain. Bonding you and your animal as one."

Once the braids are made and the candles are ready, each participant does and says the following:

<u>Participant:</u> (Taking the candle and lights it from the altar Goddess candle)

> "Ties that bind, Links that chain, together as one. Workers of the Old Religion, United in one single cause! All of One Mother, One Father, One Mystic Creation."

> "As burns this candle, so burns the walls that divide us, <u>Insert Familiars Name.</u> No longer a separate mind. Now one working mind, understanding all, caring, loving. My <u>brother/sister (appropriate gender for familiar)</u>! MY FAMILIAR!"

Now the candle is placed to the side on the altar, and the cords and the stuffed animal, (this is the animal you chose to represent the physical presence of your animal), is picked up. The Oracle hands the participant Familiar Oil. This oil is used to stroke the cord three (3) times. The participant says the following while putting the Oil on the cord:

<u>Participant:</u>

> "This oil binds our lives as one, May our works be pure and our success unlimited. This braid dedicates, consecrates, & Initiates, <u>Insert Familiar Name</u>, into the walk and work of the God & Goddess of Light.

> We are bound as one. Until such a time as one choose another walk, and our actions violate our positive beliefs. One until intentional Harm to another is done! As I have said it, Let it be so!"

Wolfen Wicca 2
Familiar Spell Page 4

The participant now ties the braid around the stuffed animals neck, and hands it to the Oracle or High Priestess. High Priestess/Oracle takes the stuffed animal and passes it through the smoke of Incense 3 times, from the left to the right.

Oracle/ High Priestess:

> "May all that has been said be so. May all your works be positive and pure. May the Lady and Lord Bless your choice! This spell has been cast, SO MOTE IT BE!"

The Oracle/High Priestess returns the stuffed animal to each of the participants. After all have done this allow the candles to burn for another 5-10 minutes. Other things may go on in the circle as the candles burn. Then put out the candles, banish the circle and clean up as usual.

*****Any left over candle can be burned again when you feel the need to "reset" the bond. The braid can be used to connect self with familiar when you are not together. It can be worn by familiar or held/worn by you.*

Lady Wolfen Mists

Wolfen Wicca 2
Class #6
Familiar Oil Recipe

© Lady Wolfen Mists Jan.1989
revised 2001

Base Oil= 50 ml of Grapeseed oil

20 drops of Vanilla
15 drop of Sandalwood
10 drops of Musk

1- 3 chips of Moonstone (optional)

Mix well together with a glass mixing stick. I like to use a glass swizzle stick, not real expensive and can be used over and over , Just clean it off with rubbing alcohol.

Allow mixed oils to sit for 3 hours as it "Marries" the scent, and place in Dark Glass Bottle, in dark place. Be sure to mark name of oil and date created on bottle

Wolfen Wicca 2
Class #6
Color Chart to refer to

© Lady Wolfen Mists Jan 22, 2015

Color Correspondence List

©By Lady Wolfen Mists 1992

This list was developed by myself, after many years of work, and gathering information. I'm not saying these are the only uses for these colors but they have been the ones that I used most frequently and with the greatest amount of success. Enjoy!

COLOR	QUALITIES
White: Represents the Virgin (maiden or youth) aspect	Use on the new moon for: virtue, sincerity, spirituality, to stabilize peace in a house, new beginnings, find truth, re-establish purity
Red: Represents the Mother (Father) aspect, Use to symbolize the God or the Fire Element. Typically used in the South Quarter	Use on the full moon for; passion, lust, sex, instill courage, increase strength & life force energy, love, Major health issues, anger issues, rid of obsessions
Pink: Represents Self-Love & discover in the growing Maiden or Youth	Use on any moon for: Finding romance, love, friendship, re-kindling affection, emotional repair, self- esteem enhancement, physical healing, women's health matters
Orange:	Use on any moon for: Stimulation in

Lady Wolfen Mists

Represents attraction in all aspects	any situation, energy enhancement, encouragement to move forward, adaptability, attraction of positive energies, listening to intuition
Yellow: Represents the Air Element. Used in the East Quarter,	Use on any moon for: Enhanced mental activity, to increase intelligence, open the gateways of the imagination, bring inspiration, develop wit & confidence
Green: Represents the Earth Element Used the North Quarter	Use on any moon for: Gaining money, wealth, success, luck, & fame Aids in developing generosity & compassion Symbol of abundance, growth, fertility, Used on the plant real for plant, tree & Earth Can be used to represent jealousy, envy, greed, desperate acts

Color Correspondence List

©By Lady Wolfen Mists 1992

Blue: Represents the Water Element Used in the West Quarter	Use on any moon for: Draw serenity & harmony, induces spiritual & mental healing. Increase psychic ability, draw inspiration from the mundane, Invoke a calmness to the area. Give open eyes to the truth, aids in finding wisdom, insures fidelity, relieves depression (especially cycle like depression)
Purple: Represents a direct line to the Higher Power or Higher self	Use on any moon for: Finding & developing a higher personal power, Produces an open & direct line to gaining an understanding of the Hidden Mysteries, gaining the Wisdom to use those powers as to benefit the entire universe. Strongly spiritual color. Gives user a code of honor to live by, increases psychic skills especially divination, Helps to rid self of addictions
Black: Represents the Crone aspect Justice aspect and War aspects	Use on the dark moon for: Increased psychic visions & dreams, can increase protective powers & shielding, Used to reverse energies in your life that are causing problems, use for un-hexing & binding, to end events, to represent death, grief & mourning, Can be used to induce discord, negative energies, confusion,

	revenge Can also be used to burn out disease from beings
Brown: represents the Earth Element can be used the North Quarter	Use on any moon for: increased business matters and success in that field, aids in finding a workable balance, used to represent self study on issues like animal magic & Earth magic Aids in decision making, stops chronic hesitation
Gray: Represent the stifled Human aspect	Use on any moon for: Relief from non-growth, feeling stuck. Aids in being neutral, cuts through the illusions of youth to the reality of life, brings on depression and feelings of confusion, being unsure of ones self and ones life experiences
Silver: Represents the Goddess, in all Her Glory and Wisdom	Use on any moon (but full moon is best) for: Permanent increase of psychic ability & power, intuition is enhanced, Draws money, wealth, success & prosperity. Gives Unconditional love and acceptance from the Goddess to the user
Gold: Represents the God, in all His splendor and enlightenment	Use on any moon (but full moon is best) for: Significant increase in money, wealth, & prosperity. Gives persuasive and influence qualities. Aids in the bettering of health. Increases divination & Spirit Warrior abilities. Gives healing to hurts & wounds of the past and includes a basic understanding of why.

Lady Wolfen Mists

Wolfen Wicca 2
Class #6
Magickal Sand Paintings

© Lady Wolfen Mists Jan.1990
revised 2001

Historically Sand Painting date back to tribal and cave dwellings days. The creation of these paintings is considered another form of spell casting, in which the caster creates an actual physical center of focus. Thus, raising a cone of power with specific end results/goals in mind. The most famous of these types of paintings are done by Tibetan Monks and Navajo Shamans. Such paintings are usually created when a healing ceremony is needed or for protection. Sand/Stone paintings are usually made/created in the form of ancient sacred symbols, or as a representation of a specific aspect of the God/dess. They may take hours or days to complete, with many intricate details. Sadly, as part of the ritual they are almost always returned to the Earth. This final act, thereby releasing all pent up energies and adding empowerment to the spell being cast.

In Wicca we also make use of the sand painting technique. The colors and meanings of colors used are fairly traditional, and these paintings can be created for just about purpose. They are to be viewed on the physical level as a focus point that will facilitate the exchange of unseen (astral) energies. Then, with the release of these energies into the universe (on the astral level) the desired end results may occur in response, on the physical level. Like traditional sand paintings, these paintings are also usually impermanent, so when the spell is sent out to the universe the painting is then returned to the Earth. All energies are released and flowing in a successful and positive manner.

However, a few sand paintings can be permanent. These types would be used for a specific purpose by a specific person within a specified space.

Wolfen Wicca 2
Class #6
Magickal Sand Paintings page 2
© Lady Wolfen Mists Jan.1990   revised 2001

For example, a protection spell for a specific person, to be used say, in a car (specific space) These paintings can, but do not have to, be made with glue for permanence. They can, but do not have to be, given to the person for them to work. They do, however, have an expiration date (for lack of better word) usually no longer then 2-3 months, at which time another painting must be constructed, if the spell is to continue.

Just a few small recommendations here if you have never created a sand painting before. Select the symbol you wish to use to represent what you are requesting before you begin the actual ritual of creation. Also choose the colors, with respect to their symbolic meanings, of sand you will be using before you begin. Another thing to be sure to do before the actual creation of the painting is to try using the sand for painting, on a "trial run". Some people separate their sand into small bottles, much like fabric paint bottles, with open ended tips so that they can have better control of the amount used. Another technique is to use filled straw or spoon to control and guide the amount of sand used. If you are working in permanent form, be sure to outline the design with some type of glue and to have that glue with you when you begin the ritual, as you may need more. I like to use the white tacky like glue to hold my sand in place but you can use what ever type you like best.

If you are having trouble with picking a sacred symbol try runes (see Rune handout). They are a wonderful source of traditional symbols one can use in sand painting. Being quite old they contain many years of powerful working energies, that can aid in successful spell casting. Also be sure when you have finished your sand painting to allow smoke for the incense on the altar to spill about it. This "sets" the energies and purifies the intentions of the caster, so that all energies and intents are in perfect harmony with the energies in the universe.

But whatever symbols you choose to use to represent your particular spell don't be afraid to go ahead and experiment! Sand paint is a skilled art and must be practiced to learn the finer techniques of creation. Discovering what works best for you is part of the creation process itself, not to mention a lot of fun!

Lady Wolfen Mists

Wolfen Wicca 2
Class #6
Symbols: Wiccan & Non-Wiccan

© Lady Wolfen Mists Jan.1990
revised 2001

Top Line: Goddess, God, Female, Male
Bottom Line: Maiden, Mother, Crone, Balefire/Needfire

Top Line: Pentagram, Horns, Ankh
Bottom Line: Cresent Moon, 8 Pointed Star, Circle

Wolfen Wicca ® Wicca 201
Class #6
Symbols: Wiccan & Non-Wiccan Page 2

Top Line: Moonrise, Moonset, Sunrise, Sunset, Spirituality, Rebirth
Bottom Line: Goddess Position, God Position, Cord

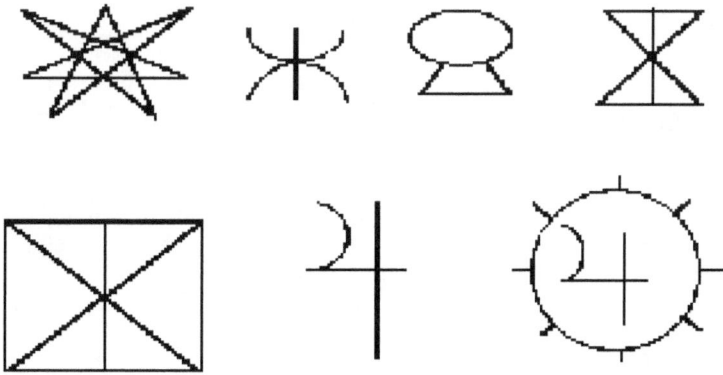

Top Line: Magickal Energy, Money, Psychic Awareness, Sex
Bottom Line: Witch Sign, To Succeed In Business, To Gain Employment

Lady Wolfen Mists

Wolfen Wicca 2
Class #6
Symbols: Wiccan & Non-Wiccan   Page 3

Top Line: Spring, Summer, Winter
Bottom Line: Autumn

Wicca 201
Class # 6
Practical: Make a Sand Painting

Instructions to the Practical Section

Use the prior instructions given, on making sand painting Mosaics, and choose a symbol you like best. Then using the sand included in this class make a sand painting . Follow the instructions given in the theory section and you should have no problems at all! Allow sand painting to dry completely, about 24 hours, before picking up You can use a symbol from class or make one up of your own, let your imagination soar & have fun. I make small pentagrams for protection or job symbols from the symbols provided anything works. Just focus, concentrate and feel the magick flow!

Notes on your Sand painting

Notes on Class 6

Lady Wolfen Mists

Wolfen Wicca 2
Our Walk Onward To Initiation
Class #7

© Lady Wolfen Mists Jan.1990
revised 2001

Theory:
Inside the circle: Reversal Polarity
Magickal Tool: The Besom
Steps to a simple Besom Chart
Wolf Protection Potpourri Recipe
Working with the stone: Onyx

Practical:
Protecting your home with onyx

Circle Work:
What is your inspirational thought for the week.

***Assignment: **Students in your Magickal Journal:**
Tell me how your Protecting your home with Onyx. How did it go? How did it feel as you were doing it, how does the energy feel now This will be reviewed when you submit your work for Initiation ☺

"I Walk On!

Wolfen Wicca 2
Class #7
Polarities & Universal Harmony

© Lady Wolfen Mists Jan.1990

Polarities those energies that keep the universe in harmony, and running smoothly. Those life sparks or charges, often called the Yin and Yang or Positive and Negativity energies. Neither charge, positive or negativity, denoting good or bad only telling of the nature of the energy!

When one is working within the realm of the physical circle, it is important to be aware of what plane/realm you are focusing your cone of power or energies upon. You already know, from 101 class, that the moon is considered a passive, negative influence on the physical plane. I'm sure you also recall that the High Priestess is the embodiment of the Goddess on the physical plane, within the circle. With that in mind it only follows that the Sun remains an active, positive influence on the physical plane. With the High Priest representing the embodiment of the God with in the physical circle.

The interaction and interdependence on each other (High Priestess & High Priest) can be exemplified in the polarization of the energies, negative and positive. On this plane of existence the

Wolfen Wicca 2
Class #7
Polarities & Universal Harmony Page 2

High Priest can only create through the use of negative passive energies of the High Priestess.

In return for this, the Universe sets up an action of balance that cause's the High Priestess to need the energies of the High Priest. Here on the physical earth bound plane, the High Priestess can only complete/finish the actual birth action, with the equal union of the positive active force know as the High Priest.

Now on Solar High days, also called Fire Sabbats, the circles energies would be considered active and positive. The reason for this is that the energies reflect the physical realm energies in the world, and at this point those energies reflect male energies. So in an effort to keep the energies balanced, the female energies (negative, passive) would be asked to cast the circle. That way a polarized balance is struck.

On Lunar (Goddess centered) times the circle is negative in polarity. Here the High Priest, or male energy, would cast the circle, to keep the polarities balanced.

Once the circle has been cast, by either based energy on the physical plane, then we (the circle and the energies therein) are on the astral plane. The astral plane causes then energies and roles that were on the physical plane to reverse. Thus the High Priestess who on the physical was negative, passive now becomes Positive & Active. The High Priest who on the physical plane was positive, active now becomes Negative & Passive in nature. So any magick done on the astral plane must reflect the energies that are dominate at that time. The female energies no longer the dreamer or inspirer it now becomes the activator and the actual act of doing. The male energies no longer the activator or the action, now becomes the thought, or the dream to be made real. I know it sounds a bit complicated but it's really not once you get the general idea in mind.

Wolfen Wicca 2
Class #7
Magickal Tool; The Besom

© Lady Wolfen Mists Jan.1990

One of the most common but least talked about magickal tools is the Besom (Broom). Just about every household today and Yesterday has one, they are easy to make, inexpensive and have a common usage. All this makes them the perfect tool, in that they can't be pointed out as a ritual tool, alone. After all years past one could/did die if accused of Witchcraft or having Witch tools. Today it's not as openly, as bad as then, but possession of ritual tools is still considered outside the "mainstream" and could cause other (non-pagans) to shun you.

Some of the more traditional uses for your besom includes sweeping the sacred circle of negativity energies. They can also be used in the same fashion to sweep your home, place of work or even your own body! Once the negativity energies have been removed the broom should be thanked, and the straws of the brooms should be dipped in salt, to help cleanse the broom.

Wolfen Wicca 2
Class #7
Magickal Tool; The Besom   page 2

Besides sweeping Besom's have a long history of non-traditional use, especially by female Witches. One such use is called "Jumping the Broom" which is preformed at Handfastings. The broom is held out in a horizontal fashion about 2 feet or so above the floor. The newly wedded couple then "jump" over it together. This act symbolizes the beginning of their new life together, their freedom from bringing any negativity influences or problems into the marriage with them, and that they are now acting as partners instead of separate people. It is also said that nothing evil (negative) can cross over a lengthwise broomstick This same broom can later be used to pep up the couples sex life, if need be. This is accomplished by placing the broom under the marriage bed, with the stick towards the head and the straws towards the foot. It's also traditionally held that Besom's are placed near the Hearth/ Fireplace of the home. The reason for this is that the Broom is able to sweep out any negative energies that might try to enter through the opening.

So as you can see, brooms can become very attached to the individual and the home itself. Your broom is yours alone and should never be shared with anyone else or loaned out. Once a broom enters its place of residence and has had a "proper" welcome, it shouldn't be moved. Even if you move to another place the Besom should be given the option to remain behind, which it probably will do, otherwise your asking for disaster and unlimited bad luck. Having more than one besom (per floor) can also cause lots of problems, drawing tons of negativity to you. As

Wolfen Wicca 2
Class #7
Magickal Tool; The Besom   page 3

you will learn, when using this magickal tool, that brooms are very territorial! But honestly, what do you think of when you think of Witches and Brooms? Could it be the Halloween Witch, (usually a ugly hag) in a conical hat, flying through the air on her broom. But it seems that one popular school of thought concerning the Witches Broom grew out of Non-Pagans misunderstanding what they may have over heard. It seems that during this period of history a Witches Broom was a slang term. This term was non flattering for women and denoted their genitals. So it follows that "riding the Witches Broom" meant more then hopping about on the corner broomstick, as you can see its meaning takes on a totally different significance when one understands the slang terms used here.

Another school of thought is based in the belief that witches mounted their broomsticks to "fly" to their Sabbats. This flying was said to be done through the use of hallucinogenic drugs, taken through a "Flying Ointment".

However I find this theory hard to give much credence to. If this ointment was used often then most of the coven members wouldn't have been able to participate in Drawing Down the Moon or any other rites or rituals. Also they would not have been able to focus clearly to achieve the altered states of consciousness need to effectively work on the astral plane or in pathworkings.

The besom is the ultimate example of the interaction/interdependence of the male & female energies, in the universe, upon each other. They are separate items that when brought together make a balanced useful working unit. The broomstick is a symbol of male energies. The straws or stalks are seen as a symbol of female energies. Each part of the broom is important in its own right and needed to complete the Besom. Within the actual Besom itself, we see that each part is unusable without the other (interdependent). Yet, when joined together (interaction), they combine to achieve the harmony and balance needed to create this magickal tool.

Lady Wolfen Mists

Wolfen Wicca 2
Class #7
Magickal Tool; The Besom   page 4

Proper care of the Besom

Taking proper care of your broom, as with all magickal tools, takes time, attention and a lot of listening to your own inner voice. After all that inner voice (intuition) has no hidden agenda and very seldom, if ever, gives us false information.

One of the first things you should do for you new Besom is to place a spell of Enchantment upon it. This aids it in "waking" giving it powerful positive energies and spiritually attuning it to your vibrational pattern. Your Besom should also have a special name. You can either ask the broom if it has something it likes to be called by, or you can give it one you feel suites it. Both of these ways are considered acceptable. The next step you might want to do is to rub down your Besom with a special Consecration Oil and consecrate it to working the ways of the Bright Lady and Lord. Attention here should be paid to the moon phase, either the waxing moon or full moon will work. Be sure that before you start the consecration you cleanse the Broom in the ritual incense smoke. If the moon phase is wrong for consecration at the time you get your Besom, then you can rub the broomstick down with a fragrant essential oil and cleanse it with Sea Salt. You should also have "birthday" celebrations for your besom. Once again the broom should be anointed with a special oil, and then cleansed in ritual smoke. Then it can be placed out in the forest over night, where it can ground and renew its energies, talk with the spirits of the forest, commune with the Bright Lady and Lord. Thus refreshing it as it was on the day of creation, or the day you brought it home.

Lastly, you need to know that there will come a time when your besom is no longer functional. The straws will be dry, brittle and broken, leaving a bigger mess then the one your trying to clean up. The handle will be cracked and splinter in your hands. The

Wolfen Wicca 20
Class #7
Magickal Tool; The Besom page 5

very "life" will be gone. When this happens you take it with you out in the forest once more. Once there you build a small fire pit and an altar of branches, big enough to place your Besom on. Next you place your dead Besom upon the altar and set fire to it. <u>Be careful to keep the flames under control, you don't want to burn anything but you broom.</u> When the fire is out and cool, take the ashes and spread them about. Once this is done, you can begin your quest to find new items, in the construction of your new Besom!

Lady Wolfen Mists

Wolfen Wicca 2
Class #7
Steps to a Besom Chart

© Lady Wolfen Mists Jan.1989
revised 2001

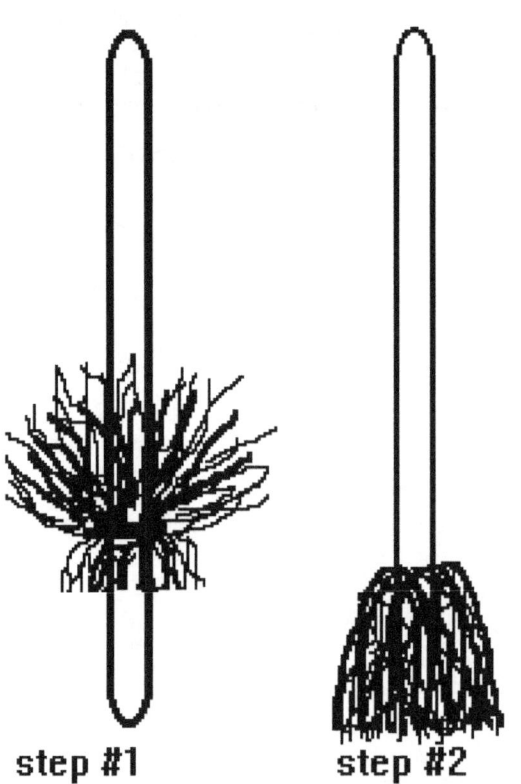

step #1
Bind straws to stick, place more at the top

step #2
Draw straws all the way down

Wolfen Wicca 2
Class #7
Steps to a Besom Chart Page 2

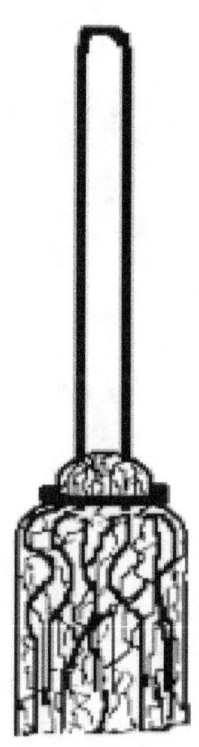

Step #3 Final step bind the top once more, tie off!

Lady Wolfen Mists

Wolfen Wicca 2
Class #7
Wolf Protection Potpourri Recipe

© Lady Wolfen Mists Jan.1990

Mix in the following ingredients:

Drop all Oils in a deosil manner (clock wise) with 12:00 at top of bowl. Drop oils around the deosil "clock." Once all is added "fold" all the ingredients together as you mix and combine the scents. Let this Potpourri sit and "Marry" for at least 3 hours before you put it all away. You can store all those in a glass bottle, canning jars work well. Plastic will allow the scent (oils) to "bleed" through and   not stay as fresh

- 1/2 cup Dried Apple Peel
- 1/2 cup Rosemary
- 1/4 cup Juniper Berries or Violet Flowers
- 1/4 cup Frankincense tears resin
- 1/4 cup Myrrh resin
- 1/2 cup Oak Moss

Mix these together well, now add in the following oils. Essentials or fragrances, what ever you can afford and like, one type of Balsam fir may not smell the same as another brand of the same scent. So be sure to smell them BEFORE you buy them. Essentials are always preferred but cost can be an issue.

Wolfen Wicca 2
Class #7
Wolf Protection Potpourri Recipe

Oils added
- 16 drops of Sandalwood Oil
- 12 droops of Myrrh Oil
- 24 drops of Dragons Blood Oil
- 12 drops of Frankincense Oil
- 6 drops of Balsam fir Oil
- 3 drops of Musk Oil

You can also make **refresher oil** for the potpourri to add as the scent begins to dissipate

Use 50 ml carrier oil (grape-seed or such)
- 16 drops of Sandalwood Oil
- 12 droops of Myrrh Oil
- 24 drops of Dragons Blood Oil
- 12 drops of Frankincense Oil
- 6 drops of Balsam fir Oil
- 3 drops of Musk Oil

Mix all together and store in a dark place in a dark (amber is good) glass bottle. Measure out in 2 dram bottler to give away as refresher oils to potpourri

Lady Wolfen Mists

Wolfen Wicca 2
Class #7
Working with the Stone; Onyx

© Lady Wolfen Mists Jan.1990

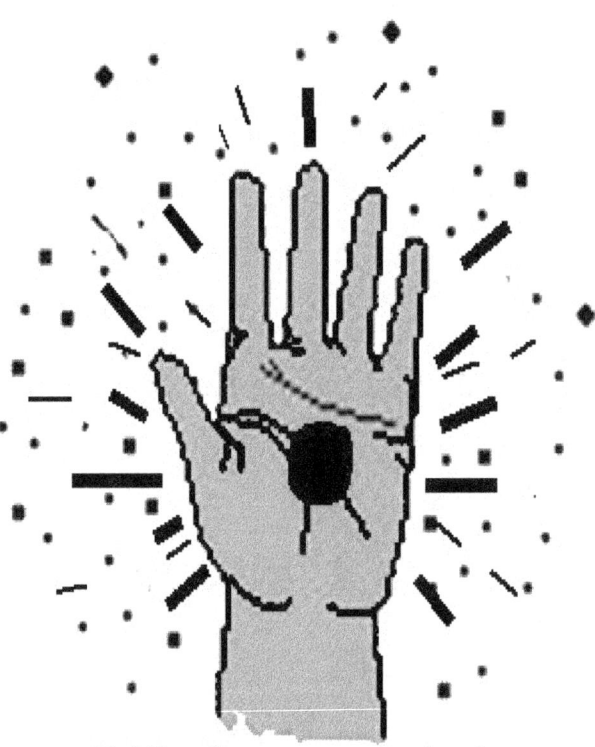

Holding Onyx can cause rips & tears in aura

    Black Onyx is a very strong stone and can cause MUCH damage if not used correctly. This stone should only be attempted to be used by an extremely advanced "stone Worker". This practitioner must have a "higher" purpose in mind or there could be lasting damage, to the patient, caused by this stone.

    Always when using ONYX, use it together/ in conjunction. with a piece of APACHE TEAR. This stone helps to balance the energies of the Onyx and lends a healing aura to any misdirected energies that might be emitted. Apache Tear, is a light in the darkness, and keeps us in touch with the Higher Spiritual energies that surround us in everyday life. It acts as a minor healer, major protector, and a life saver when used with powerful stones. When not in use Onyx should always be stored in red as it resonates at the root chakra level.

    Now I hope you have the picture that this stone is not one to play with! But many of you who wish to become a stone worker/ healer will want to learn to use this stone. So here are a few pointers that will keep you safe as you learn to use this stone in a successful manner.

Wolfen Wicca 2
Class #7
Working with the Stone; Onyx page 2

1. Onyx is known to "open" holes in the etheric body/ aura. This is good if there is a negative area that needs dissipated in the aura, such as an unwanted hook from someone to you or a curse. Using Onyx on that area, because it's to deep to remove any other way, causes the area to be punctured and "psychic bleeding" can occur. Psychic bleeding feels like that run down feeling, the one where you have slept all night but still feel tired, beat up and achy. Apache Tear is used to help in closing these types of holes, and to even out the energy involved.

2. Onyx is used to help enhance visions. Again it is important to take care in using this, as these types of vision can become painfully powerful, and to jumbled up to understand fully. Again **Apache Tear is used along with EMERALD**, to calm the mind and allow the image to flow as smoothly and as clearly as it takes for the mind to accept them. **HEMATITE should be included also,** so that complete and total recall of visions can be enhanced. Small pieces, such as those found in rings and other jewelry items, can be worn to tap into others thoughts. Yet the user should be made aware that this can become too much and cause serious health problems, in the least headaches or at the most permanent brain damage.

3. Onyx is great to use as a medium in which to instill or add something into the etheric body. However when doing this extra caution needs to be used, as the entire etheric body is put <u>at risk</u>, and real damage can take place by an untrained, unskilled worker.

So please before you use Onyx be sure to have a special piece of Apache Tear that is used only with it. Do not use this stone to experiment with!!! If you chose to use this stone in your healing practice, be sure that you have an experienced Stone worker train you, and be sure you are ready for the responsibility involved when using this stone.

Say WHAT? I Could be Puttin' Holes in ME?
Yikes !

Wolfen Wicca 2
Class #7
Practical: Protecting your self and Home with a Black Onyx Charm

© Lady Wolfen Mists Jan.1990

Below is the general overall outline used for the practical section of this class. I've included this so if you have a specific question you can go directly to that section and find the answer quickly. I hope you find it helpful.

1. Purpose:
2. Items Included:
3. Special Information:
4. Steps to Preparation:
5. Special Storage Needs:
6. Clean Up:
7. Recharge Procedure

1) Creating this charm aids you in being able to tell the truth. It is used to give you clear sight into whatever someone might be speaking about, kind of like a lie detector. Its second purpose is to protect the surroundings. Keeping any negative energies that may have been directed to you, while keeping your mind clear and free from any unwanted connections to the crown and 3rd eye chakra.

Lady Wolfen Mists

Wolfen Wicca 2
Class #7
Practical: Protecting your self and Home with a Black Onyx Charm Page 2

2)

Items to collect for this class	Additional Items Needed
1 small container with a lid	*Things to decorate container, Anything goes*
1 piece of Black Onyx	*Any herbs for protection you may wish to add IE Basil, Bay Laurel, Mistletoe, Myrrh, Oak, Roses, Rowan, Yarrow*
1 Apache Tear	Holy Water- If you don't have metaphysical correct Holy water use bottled water with a pinch of Sea salt added (its not the best but it will work)
1 packet Wolf Protection Potpourri	
Sea Salt	

3) Create this charm at night after 5:00 pm. When finished let set in the moonlight for at least 4-8 hours, then put in sunlight for another 4-8 hours. Once this is completed its ready to use!

4) **Steps: Be sure to cast a regular circle when creating this charm**
    1. Cleanse container and stones with Metaphysically Holy Water or Sea Salt. Allow them to remove any energies that may have been placed there before the items got to you.

    2. Lay out all the items that you will be using in front of you, so that you will have easy access to them.

    3. Next begin to decorate your container, it can be however you like, just remember its most likely to be in public view. I like to use a magickal theme with most of my items, but its not necessary for the charm to work. You can decorate it to fit in with any decor. This charm can also be made as a gift, great for birthdays or Yule, so think about the person you might be giving it to.

    4. Once the container is done, dry from any paint or glue, you're ready for the next step. Now add the packet of Wolf Protection Potpourri to your container while Saying the following;

Wolfen Wicca 2
Class #7
Practical: Protecting your self and Home with a Black Onyx Charm Page 3

> "May these Herbs, grown in the fertile soil of the Mothers heart.
> Guide and protect me in the way of Truth and Light"

Now add the Black Onyx and Apache Tear saying the following;

> "May these stones, born of the furnace of the Fathers passions,
> Keep my heart and mind safe
> Keep my spirit clear."

****Now you may add any additional herbs or oil here if you want. Next hold up the charm to each of the 4 directions. Say the following, once to each direction;

> "This little charm made by me,
> My home made safe for all to see.
> Air, fire water and Earth,
> Keep negativity away, dispersed.
> So Mote It Be!"

So you are done with your charm. All that's left is to banish the circle in the normal manner and clean up.

5) Nothing special

6) Clean up as usual

7) No need to repower this charm up as the energies continue to naturally repower itself. But if you feel the need to clean it just add a drop or two of Holy water to the potpourri mixture or a pinch or two of Sea Salt. place lid on jar/charm and shake. When you are finished you can take the lid off the jar again.

Notes on your Practical

Notes on Class 7

Lady Wolfen Mists

Wolfen Wicca 2
Our Walk Onward To Initiation
Class #8

© Lady Wolfen Mists Jan.1990
revised 2001

Theory:
Explain the Ten (10) planes
Explain the Tree of Life
Weather Magick
Wind Chart
Air Oil Recipe
Weather Working Dust recipe
Weather Magick- Omens Chart

Practical:
Storm Magick Spell: Whistle Up the Wind

Circle Work:
What is your inspirational thought for the week.

***Assignment: **Students in your Magickal Journal**:
Do the Storm Magick spell and submit a **complete** report how it went for you. Was it a success? How could you tell? Was it not a successful spell? Where do you think it went wrong? What can you do to improve the spell and make it more "personal"? This will be reviewed when you submit your work for Initiation ☺

"I Walk On!"

Wolfen Wicca 2
Class #8
Kabbalah: Tree of Life

© Lady Wolfen Mists 1992

Kabbalah is an ancient Magickal system based on the esoteric interpretations of the **Hebrew Scriptures**. It contains many ways or tools to help the user reach a oneness or union with the God figure. One of the main tools in this system of magick is the Tree of Life.

Although it should be pointed out that the use of the **Tree of Life is not traditional Wiccan practice**, it is seen and used a lot by practitioners of magick in this day and age. As such I felt that you should at least have a basic knowledge of the Tree of Life, its meanings and uses. If you choose to use it or not use it in your practice, its up to you.

The Tree of Life is considered a systematic, organized way to work, interact and understand the Universe as a whole. It explains the evolution of all things, with special emphasis on the Universe, and all the energies within it.

It is said that the creator grew through a series of stages all growing on the next. That there were nine (9) stages of evolution until the tenth (10th), which is the physical, completed it development. The tenth is considered the last and final level of evolution. The stages as a whole, were said to become more and more specialized, yet they were all a branch off the same tree, the same original energy.

Thus the Tree of Life consists of ten (10) spheres called the Ten Holy Sephiroth (Sef-Fur-Roth). Interconnecting with these spheres are twenty two (22) lines called <u>paths.</u> Together, the spheres and paths, make up the <u>thirty two (32) Paths of Wisdom</u>.

Each one of the individual Sephiroth represents one of the states of Consciousness. These conscious states contain our abilities and energies. Each one of the sephira(a single sphere) is considered to be a specific stage in the creation of the universe. They were created or evolved from nothingness to the physical plane, where we as humans exist. These levels can also be found within our own self, as levels within our own physical development. Each sephira share and builds on the abilities, energies and forces of the previous ones. This type of building, with use of these powers, in evolution has a special name also. This name is the <u>Path of the Flaming Sword.</u>

Each one of the Sephira also has a Divine name, an aspect of the Christian God and an Order of Angels or Archangels, found therein. The Order of Angels or Archangels duty is to teach protection, and guide you on your personal growth journey.

Kabbalah: Tree of Life
Page 2

Levels of the Sephiroth

1. **Malkuth**

    The first of the Sephira is named Malkuth. This is a sphere that is closest to our waking consciousness. It is the level that is closest and affects our physical, daily, life. The Divine name here is <u>Adonoi Ha Aretz</u> (Ah-Doe-Nigh-Ha-Ah-Ratz), meaning "Lord of the Earth and Visible Universe" Many, many angels are assigned to and can be contacted from this sphere. The main and easiest angel to speak with here would be <u>Sandalphon.</u> He is known as the Approacher. It is his job to take your prayers to those beings who can best answer them. The <u>Ashim</u> or Souls and Flames of the Fires, are under his direction here, These are those blessed souls who work closely on the earth plane. Here you also experience and learn the reality of the Devas and Fairy Folk.

2. **Yesod**

    The second level is called Yesod. It is considered the foundation of the Etheric/Astral planes, and is closely associated with the moon. This is considered to be the gateway to all the planes. The God aspect here is <u>Shaddai El Chai.</u>, meaning "Almighty Living God". It is here we gain some idea of the plan of the Universe. The Angel in charge here is, <u>Archangel Gabriel</u>. He is considered the angel of truth and chief of the guards placed over paradise. The Cherubim or Strong Ones, are under his direction, and they tend the Akashic Records. They are known as the angels of light and Glory, Keepers of the Celestial Records.

Kabbalah: Tree of Life
Page 3

3. ### Hod

    The third level is called Hod. Hod teaches learning, communications, trade, commerce and exchange of ideas. Here you can learn about Materialization and Dematerialization. The God aspect here is <u>Elohim Tzabaoth</u>, meaning "God of Host, ruling the universe in Wisdom and Harmony". This level reveals scientific and general knowledge. The Archangel is <u>Micheal.</u> He is Prince of Splendor and wisdom, the great Protector. On this level are the Beni Elohim, meaning Children of Gods. Their main job is to instill you with the overwhelming drive and need to know and recognize Gods will and work with them.

4. ### Netzach

    The fourth level is Netzach. Netzach is full of emotions and beauty and teaches you how to work with them. It is at this level you need to be cautious of being "Fairy Charmed" and not being able to see things in perspective. The God aspect here is <u>Jehova Tzabaoth</u>, meaning "God of Hosts". Here God is seen as a higher form of expression of emotion & unconditional Love. The Archangel her is female and called <u>Haniel</u>. She is the Archangel of grace, love, harmony & patron of the Arts. The Elohim (minor Gods and Goddess) work together here under her charge. They are sent to take care of many other duties found in other religions. They are called to be protectors of religion.

5. ### Tiphareth

    The fifth level is called <u>Tiphareth.</u> Tiphareth teaches healings, higher teachers, abundance and success. The God aspect here is called <u>Jehova Aloah Va Daath</u>, meaning "God of all Knowledge and Wisdom." The Archangel here is <u>Raphael</u>, who is known as the angel of brightness, healing, life & beauty. He is also called the Healer of God. Working under his direction are the Malachim or Messengers. They are said to give valor, grace, and honor to individuals. They are also the ones who work miracles upon the Earth physical plane.

6. Geburah

The sixth level is called Geburah. On Geburah you will find greater energy, courage, initiative, judgment and making room for changes. The God aspect here is called Elohim Gibor, meaning "God Almighty". The Archangel in charge here is Kamael, also called Prince of Strength, Courage & Severity. Working under his direction are the Seraphim, or Flaming Ones, Fiery Serpents. Their job is to give us the power to overthrow those who would send us negative energies.

7. Chesed

The seventh level is called Chesed. Here you will find peace, organization, mercy, growth, prosperity. The god aspect here is El, meaning "Mighty One". The Archangel in charge here is Tzadkiel also called Prince of Mercy & Justice. He works with those called the Brilliant ones also known as the Chasmalim. It is there job to aid you in a clear understanding of the Majesty of God.

8. Binah

The eighth sphere is called Binah. Here patience & understanding is found. The God aspect is Jehova Elohim meaning "God of Gods." It is here we find understanding of life and all the areas within. The Archangel Tzaphkiel, also called Prince of Spiritual Strife against Evil, the contemplation of God Under his charge are the Aralim, the strong and Mighty ones, the Thrones. They are known for there interrelationship between Mother Earth & our actions. They are appointed to look out for all things on the Earth.

9. Chokmah

The ninth level is called Chokma. It is here that wisdom is learned, and the Divine Light, filtered over from the 10th sphere, can be found. The God aspect here is Yah or Jah, meaning Divine Ideal wisdom. The Archangel in charge here is Ratziel, also called Prince of

Kabbalah: Tree of Life
Page 4

Hidden Knowledge & Concerned Things, Herald of Deity, the Wheels. Those under his charge are the Auphanim or Whirling Forces, they allow you the spiritual experience of finally seeing the face of God, actually being in His physical presence.

10. **Kether**

The tenth (10th) and final sphere is Kether. This is the deepest level, closest to the pure white light. It is the first (1st) sphere that developed out of nothingness. This is the last level that exists before being fully reunited with God. The God aspect here is <u>Eheieh</u>, meaning "I Am that I Am". The Archangel at this level is <u>Metatron</u>, who is the greatest of all angelic beings, Angel of Presence. His job is to aid and sustain humankind. Under his charge are the Chaioth Ha Qudesh seraphim, also called the Holy Living Creatures. Their jobs include helping us to understand your spiritual growth, evolutionary process and the Kabbalah

Quick fact overview

The Tree of Life is said to show the standard Astral realms that one can 'rise" to. Kabbalah traditionally accepts ten (10) standard realms, of which the first four (4) <u>must</u> be traveled completely at least once. Once these first four (4) have been travelled though in their completeness, at least once, then the practitioner can "skip" to the next levels, without having to spend time in the first four (4) if they choose not to. The last three (3) realms of this Tree must always be traveled in succession, each and every time, due to the nature or content of what they contain. Other spellings for Kabbalah include: Qabbalah, Kabala, Cabbalah, Cabala.

Lady Wolfen Mists

Wolfen Wicca 2
Class #8
Tree of Life: Kabbalah

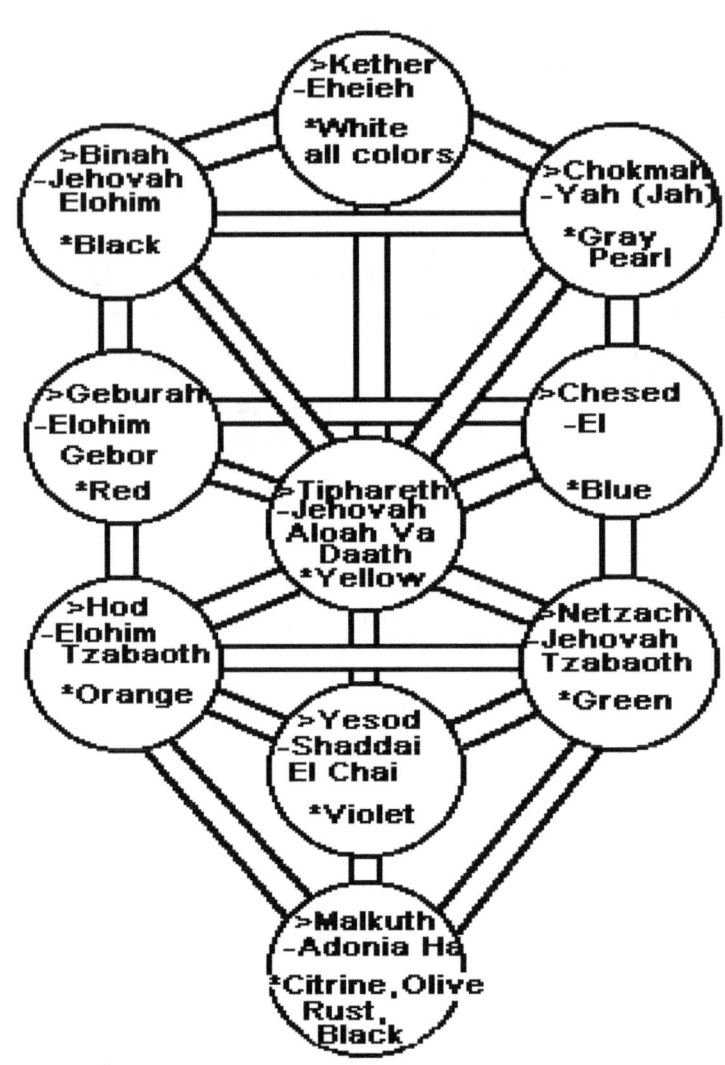

KEY:
- **> Name of the Sephiroth**
- **- God Name/Aspect**
- *** Sephiroth Color/Candle Color**

Wolfen Wicca 2
Class #8
Tree of Life: Kabbalah Archangel

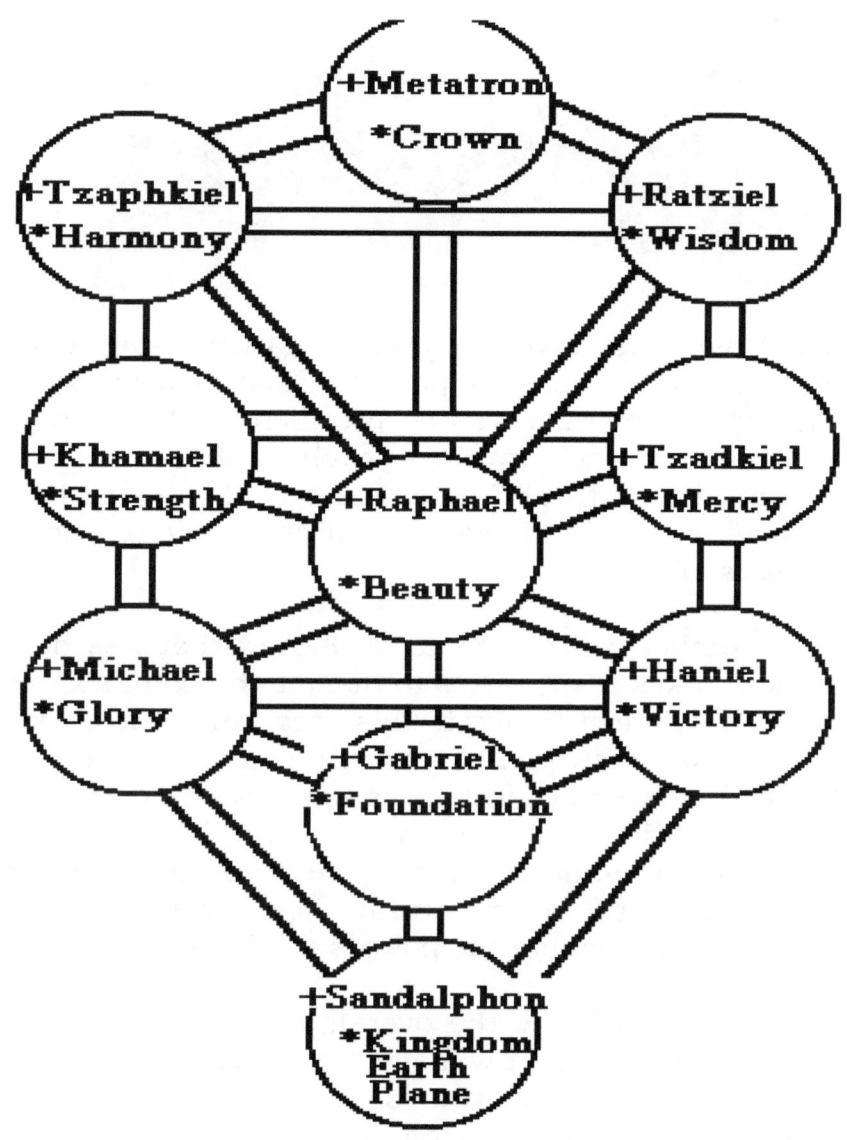

KEY:
+ = Archangel in charge
* Level of Consciousness-Main idea in this Sephira

Lady Wolfen Mists

Class #8
Introduction to Weather Magick

© Lady Wolfen Mists Jan.1990

Weather Magick is a very powerful natural source of cosmic energy. Bending, weaving or manipulating this power has always been seen as one of the skills a witch possessed. The belief was so prevalent in the middle ages that there was actual laws that forbade anyone (witches) from controlling, tampering, harnessing or changing the natural flow or pattern of the weather. Some laws also forbade women from whistling, as all women but especially old women, were thought of as natural controllers of weather.

Would be weather controllers need to know that weather magick is a hard won skill, and as such, takes many years to master the complexities therein. But if you are one of the ones who feel drawn to this area, and you insist on trying "your hand" in this area, here are a few pointers to help you get started. These pointers are just that, POINTERS! They are not all there is to know, they are not even considered a scratch on the surface of the information you need to become a master in this area. They are however, a general guide to try and see if you are attracted to this type of magick, or if you even have a flare or natural talent for this area. Please remember this when you attempt to manipulate the powers of the weather.

1. Take time to get to know the overall weather trends, especially those in your area, as those are the ones that will effect you most. Understand how you react to those trends or changes? How does your body react to those same changes trends? For example when it rains does your ankle hurt or swell?

2. You must learn to visualize well, being able "see" and interpret the many changes going on around you. You also need to be able to interpret the possible changes that these trends may be bringing your way.

Class #8

Wolfen Wicca 2; Our Walk Onward To Initiation

Introduction to Weather Magick Page 2

3. Hone you skills of observation. Be able to observe the wild life in the area and your own pets. Notice what their behavior is like during specific weather trends. For example, do they hide before a rainstorm? Do they "talk" or more than normal before a thunderstorm or snowstorm?

4. Be able to faithfully spend at least fifteen to twentyfive (15-25) minutes a day outside in the weather. There you will need to ground yourself, commune with the powers/energies of nature, and the powerful energies of the universe that set the course of the weather.

5. Lastly on the pointers list, you will need to become more sensitive. This includes, on a daily basis, any smells, sounds, colors, feelings or emotions that the changes in weather bring out in you, and all those around you. All humans, plant life and animal life need to be considered in this area. Complete knowledge in this area will ensure success in any weather magick spells that you may cast!

So if you follow the above pointers in full, and become fairly proficient at them, you will have a very basic foundation from which to build. However I'm sure you can now see how very intense and difficult it is to become a skilled practitioner of this specialty. The focus one needs and the research involved, combined with the actual hands on work, amounts to many many years of continuous and devout study! I don't want you to think I'm trying to warn you away from this area, I just don't want to mislead you. I don't want you to think this area of magick is one you can take a week-end seminar, and then consider yourself a master practitioner. It does takes tons of work, research and experience to achieve a significant level of competency. But for the witch who achieves the skills as a master in this area, all the years of work and study, have been worthwhile indeed.

Lady Wolfen Mists

Wolfen Wicca 2
Class #8
Wind Chart for working with the Weather and Wind

© Lady Wolfen Mists Jan.1990

Direction	Qualities of Wind	Easiest time to call up
North Wind	Cold & Wet & Biting	Winter
East Wind	Cold & Dry	Spring
South	Warm & Dry	Summer
West	Warm & Wet	Autumn

Wolfen Wicca 2
Class #8
Air Oil

© Lady Wolfen Mists march 1991

Mix these Ingredients together and let sit overnight to "marry" the scents together. This is a smaller batch so it wont go bad as quickly. This oil is best when "freshly" made

1/8 cup of Grapseed Oil

7 drops of Lavender
2 drops of Sweet Orange Oil
4 drops of Sandalwood oil
1 drop Lemon Oil
5 drops of Orris Oil or Musk

"Sending out your will and letting it Hang in the Air. Reaching out to the Universe"

Lady Wolfen Mists

Wolfen Wicca 2
Class #8
Weather working Dust

© Lady Wolfen Mists May 2003

Mix these Ingredients together first
- 1/4 cup of Arrowroot Powder
- 15 drops of Oak Moss Oil

Next mix together the following ingredients on top of above mixture

1/4 cup Chinchilla dust (ask for it at any pet store, it is used by chinchillas to roll in and dust their selves off with)

6 Tablespoons of dirt. (potting soil works well if its that time of year you cant get dirt due to snow)

1/4 cup of Borage Leaf

1/4 cup of shredded Dandelion flower or crushed Rose petals

Weather working Dust Page 2

    Next Place the completed Mixture in a bag and shake intensely. While shaking it focus energy on the wind elemental. "See" it entering your mixture and storing its energies there. Do this for not just this dimension but for all those other open door positive energy dimensions. "See" them Living within this dust, as it is now belonging to the elemental of wind, and contains many many sparks of creation on many many different levels and dimensions. I know that sounds easy but the focus energy you need for so many dimension is much harder than thought. It has much to do with visualization and recalling all the Open Doors " you have been through (astral wise) or physically, and placing those energies gathered from there into this dust, thus imbuing it with all your experiences and your ancestors as well. It takes time and wisdom as well as experiences to make a really really great dust so don't be discouraged if yours seems a bit at first, it will get stronger with practice from you in making this. Please store this in a leather or cloth bag which will be used for nothing else but this dust

Lady Wolfen Mists

Wolfen Wicca 2
Class #8
Weather Magick: Omens & Old Wives Tales

© Lady Wolfen Mists Jan.1990

Indicators of :Storms: On the way

-Cats sitting with their backs to the fire place or door
-Blue flames in a fireplace
-Dogs rolling on the ground
-Horses/cows standing in a group away from the hedge
-Spiders destroying their webs
-Shooting Stars
-Wolves howling

Indicators of :Good Weather

-Robins singing on high places (i.e. Barns)
-New Spider webs in the morning
-Warm winds blowing from the west
-Squirrels eating in the trees
-Birds flying high in the sky
-Rainbow at evening
-Red lightening---Red sky at night
-Clouds that look like wool

Wolfen Wicca 2
Class #8
Weather Magick: Omens & Old Wives Tales Page 2

Indicators of :Rain

-Rainbows in the afternoon
-Cats sneezing
-Ants hiding
-Bees staying inside the hive
-Leaves showing their back to you
-Dark mist over the moon
-Red sky at morning
-A ring around the moon
-Smoke not going out the chimney
-Flower & grass smell stronger than normal

Indicators of : Hard Winter coming

-Late first frost
-Tough, thick apple skins
-Trees keeping their leaves longer than usual for the season
-Lots of acorns on the ground and stored by squirrels
-Weeds growing high into the season
-Moss growing heavy on trees
-Birds huddling together and on the ground
-Birds foraging for food
-Thicker than average fur on all animals

Wolfen Wicca 2
Class #8
Weather Magick: Whistle Up the Wind Spell

©by Lady Wolfen Mists c 1996

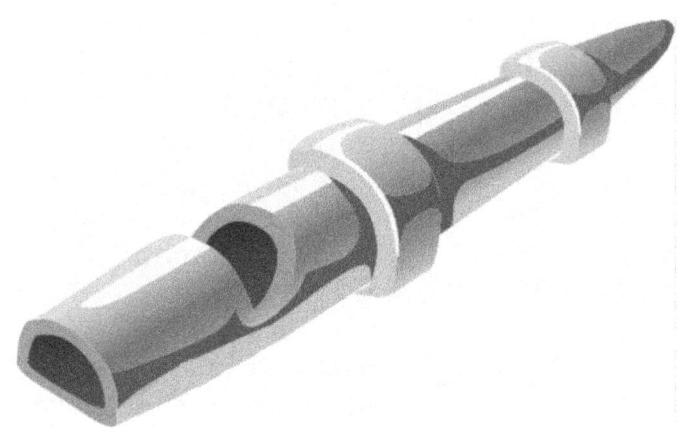

The following is a spell to help you learn to whistle up the wind. It is listed in steps so that you can better follow it. Also remember, don't feel bad if it takes awhile to get the reaction you want. Mastering weather takes perseverance. ***There are no special items needed for this spell except a whistle.***

1. Stand at the highest point you can safely find, like a hill top.

2. Face the direction (see wind chart) you want to call the wind from. Visualize the watchers/elements that live in that particular direction. See "them" approaching through their open gate, bringing their qualities and attributes with them. Riding the very winds that you are calling, coming to you!

3. While visualizing the above and while facing the direction, raise both arms up. Hold them over your head, palms facing forward and outward. Next pull the energies from within the Earth up through your feet, growing in power until they reach your hands.

4. As this is happening allow the energies to build to your throat. Begin to allow the energies to vocalize, the sound building and rising to a sharp cry, as the powers raise within yourself.

Wolfen Wicca 2; Our Walk Onward To Initiation

Class #8
Weather Magick: Whistle Up the Wind Spell Page 2

5. Once the energies have reached your hands and the sound "feels" ready to send out, then release the energies. Try to this in one loud long yell, if possible. sending the energies and tone out to the direction you want to call.

6. If you feel your will was successfully sent in the vocalization, then blow three (3) long sets of three (3) on your whistle. I like using an oak whistle but any type will do.

7. When you have completed the above steps, stand silently, arms at your sides. Breath deeply, awaiting the on rush of wind that you have called up. Like I said before, don't feel bad if it doesn't work exactly as described. As I warned before it does take lots of constant focus, visualization and <u>practice.</u> Another thing you might want to do at the beginning, when your trying to figure out if you raised <u>any</u> wind at all, is to hang a chime above you. One that has a pleasant yet distinctive sound, that will be sure to catch your attention, when ringing from the whisper of the wind.

Using Weather Working Dust

When you are trying and trying and cant seem to get the energies to cooperate there is always the option of using Weather Working Dust, which can be used in place of the Whistle to aid in calling up the wind energies. **<u>Follow the spell above to step 6, then get ready to use the Weather Working Dust in place of the Whistle:</u>**

6. If you feel your will was successfully sent in the vocalization, then toss four (4) pinches of Weather Working Dust into the air around you. Let it ride the winds about you and see the energies delivering your will to the universe as you sent it. This dust acts as a marker that you have completed the spell and have sent the energies you called up out to the universe. It gets the Universes attention that you have created your spell, focused your energies, sent it out and as the dust rides the currents, all WILL BE SO!

7. When you have completed the above steps, stand silently, arms at your sides. Breath deeply, awaiting the on rush of wind that you have called up.

Class #8
Weather Magick: Whistle Up the Wind Spell Page 3

Just a quick note: Weather Working Dust is easy to use but very energy intensive to create or find. It takes someone who is well acquainted with the Laws of both this universe and other dimensions, but who also understands the dimension of the Spirits of Nature. So treasure what you have, but I caution you it should be used sparingly. This is indeed the **_real thing_** and it positively does send out, to those who are gifted with this weather work ability, the thoughts and energies of this spell. As such the results can be truly astounding!

Notes for Class 8

Lady Wolfen Mists

Wolfen Wicca 2
Class #9

© Lady Wolfen Mists Jan.1990
revised 2001

Theory:

Amulets & Talismans & General Overall Information
Faery Trivia
The Four (4) Elements
The Four (4) Elements Chart
Magickal Wells
Samhain: Overview of Traditions
Samhain Sabbat with Information on Talisen in brief

Practical:
Do a normal Circle casting & Invoke Talisen into your circle

Circle Work:
What is your inspirational thought for the week.

***Assignment: <u>**Students in your Magickal Journal**</u>:

Do Circle Casting and Invoke Talisen. Use the ritual included as a guide, it is for a group but you can convert it to solitary. Report what you were inspired to create during this time. What did the Circle feel like at this time? How did you feel? This will be reviewed when you submit your work for Initiation ☺

"I walk on"

Wolfen Wicca 2
Class #9
Difference between Talisman & Amulet
& Other Odds and Ends

© Lady Wolfen Mists 1992

This is a witch amulet often carried to draw other witches to you and to keep your power clean and safe free from negative energies

Personal point on this subject

Ya know what drives me crazy? Well yes lots of things, but tonight it is something in particular. Its "Wicca wanna be sellers at auctions." I have just came from several on line auction places and have been looking at things to buy (I like buying things and on line shopping is about the only way I can shop anymore.) OK so anyway I get to the sites and I see Amulets and Talismans. So I go to them thinking I have found a real treasure, maybe a practitioner of many years who is making real amulets and talismans to share with others...Ohhh I am so excited at my find.

I open the sellers page and what do I find??? Oh about 30 amulets listed. OK I think that's a lot of work and programming but maybe they have been hoarding them for some time. So I give them the benefit of the doubt and click again.....Humm I think I wonder what type of amulets they have for sale??? I look at the page, its NO AMULET! It's a Smokey quartz stone set in a necklace, cheap setting at that with a huge price tag. The description doesn't mention a thing about its programming and it only lists its natural properties as a stone! I scream..Not again!

Again and again I find this all over the auction on the web and in the other young Wiccans I see (as well as some older ones) these are Book Wiccans. They have read the popular pagan writer of the month or some other such and are now tried and true knowledgeable Wiccans, who need no more direction as they have complete every book published in the last 4 months of a particular publisher and are now ready to teach. They don't believe in ranking systems hummm I wonder why, as they are not

Class #9
Difference between Talisman & Amulet
& Other Odds and Ends Page 2

are not even Initiated and are now a self reveled 3rd degree at 20 years old. They have by the way no idea what the difference between an Amulet or a Talisman is and really don't care. They know what such items are as they have used them forever in their role playing D & D games, (not to knock role playing as I have spent a few nights myself there) and KNOW that they are natural Wiccans and they don't need any training in the Craft.

Ok so maybe this kind of thought wouldn't bother me so much **IF** it just influenced them and their path...but here they are on auction sites, where people (many times beginners) come looking for legitimate items. The sellers portray themselves as these wonderful 3rd degrees and Spiritual adviser's, yet they don't even know what a Amulet or a Talisman is (the very basic of magickal tools) and are selling this crap as TRUE MAGICKAL TOOLS!!! Now Beginners are buying into it, not only the items, thinking they are real magickal amulets but into the ideas such Wicca wanna bees project!

Oh where has stepping out of the dark shadows brought us, I ask you. Are we not the favorite "fad" religion going, greed has overshadowed the beauty of the journey and the magick of discovery. Many have no idea what its like to sit at there foot of your teacher as She shares her secrets and insights with you, these bits of treasure hard won by her over the years. Many have no idea how wonderfully enjoined it feels to hear from the High Priest the views of males in the craft and the beauty they share at their relationship with the Goddess. The interaction is not there any more, the knowledge is not honored, the tradition of handing down is dismissed and the achievement status of earning a rank after putting in many hours of work is denied important.

Instead this new fad religion promises that after reading 150 odd pages of written tripe you to can call yourself a High Priestess and if you buy the next 2 books you too can develop into a 3rd degree. Hell if you buy this wonderful other book on tarot you can be a Master Tarot reader in, oh say, 30 minutes by following 7 easy steps and forking over $19.99. Goddess what have we allowed our religion to develop into!

Not everything comes just because we think it should, sometimes the journey is much more important that the destination, like growing into a High Priestess or High Priest. It is the many forms of experience that comes with it, the learning of tidbits of knowledge at the knees of someone who has studied and worked daily at her/his craft. Not how many books they have read, not how quickly they absorbed the knowledge (cause that's no big deal its there for anyone and everyone who wants to take it) but the weave of the journey. The dark spots, the light ones, the mistakes

Class #9
Difference between Talisman & Amulet
& Other Odds and Ends Page 3

made and the success earned. The laughter and loves, all the wonders found in between. These people KNOW what a true magickal tool is and that they share that with those who want to learn and not just label or call something such because it sounds cool and will draw in bidders and bring them a pretty penny...These are the people who deserve our respect and our acknowledgment. They are the Ancient Jewels of our community. All others should do like the song says and *Hit the road Jack and dont ya come back, no more, no more. no more, no more*... please just think on it a bit.

Anyway that's what drives me nuts tonight. Oh for those who don't know here is a brief definition of the two terms

What is an Amulet,
Its a Magickal tool that is made for a **general purpose that anyone can use,** it is passive in that anyone can pick it up and use it, there is seldom magickal activation needed of these types of tools. They are ready to use when found or given to you. For example it's like a general all around programmed money amulet, that is usually worn or carried to bring money to the wearer.

This magickally empowered item is usually used to deflect energies. It is a **general overall item,** meaning that it is not designed for one person in particular but for anyone's use. It's traditionally used to stop or negate negative energies from reaching the user. It is usually worn but can be placed in an area to protect that area. Tattoos can be used as a permanent Amulet or Talisman.

What is a Talisman
A Talisman is another type of magickal tool that is **created for a specific person for a specific purpose**. No one else can use it unless it is passed on and it usually has words of activation. An example of this would be an item (worn or carried) programmed specifically for say our friend Robin. The purpose of Robin's special tool (talisman) would say, to be to make their acting unforgettable in a positive way, so this magickal tool would be created just for Robin. For just for that purpose and have some part of Robin invested in it (a clipping of hair or such used in the creation process! There are usually very special words of activation with a talisman and can only be used by others if the Talisman is handed down by the original owner or if the Talisman chooses a new owner after the other has crossed the veils.

Class #9
Difference between Talisman & Amulet
& Other Odds and Ends Page 3

Overall it is an empowered item that has been charged/programmed **to attract a specific set of energies**, like to get a specific job. It is usually made for one person in particular and is not a general use item. A talisman is normally worn but can be an object that sets or hangs somewhere.

Please Note: Any stones or metals or woods used in either of these items add the natural abilities to the programming but these alone **DO NOT** constitute an amulet or talisman, it needs to be programmed, period!

Blessings as another night turns by,
Lady Wolfen Mists

Other Odds and Ends

FFF or 777- This is an Old Wiccan Blessing meaning,
- Flags (flagstone dwelling place)
- Flax (clothing)
- Fodder (food).

A 4th F can be used for Freya, the Goddess of Hearth and Home

To keep away negative energies from taking over your home, just hang bunches of seaweed throughout the house. Tie bunches in red, white and purple ribbon.

When doing a candle spell be sure to freeze the candles that you plan to use prior to the spell casting, this ensures the candles will burn longer and more evenly.

Finding a stone that is naturally round with a natural hole in it is a gift from the Goddess. This type of stone is sacred and will bring the finder a "boon". Be sure to keep the stone for all time to meditate on and wish on.

If in your change, you find a coin with your birth date on it keep it. It is extremely lucky and will act as a charm of abundance.

Wolfen Wicca 2; Our Walk Onward To Initiation

Difference between Talisman & Amulet
& Other Odds and Ends Page 4

When carrying cash (bills) in your pocket or wallet be sure to fold the bills towards you. This continues to bring money to you. If you fold them away from you then the energies will flow the opposite way, losing money for you.

Did you know that Hecate was the sole Titan who was allowed to keep her powers under the rule and leadership of Zeus.

Days of the Week & Their Significance

Day of Week	Ruling Planet	Magickal Properties
Sunday	Sun	Success, Fame Strength, Protection, Healing,
Monday	Moon	Peace, Psychic abilities, Purification, Compassion
Tuesday	Mars	Sex, Passions, Causes, Survival, Courage, Anger
Wednesday	Mercury	Divination, Wisdom, Travel, Spiritual Study
Thursday	Jupiter	Money, Prosperity, Success, Abundance, flow
Friday	Venus	Love, Beauty, Arts, Friendship. Renewal, Marriage
Saturday	Saturn	New Houses, Travel, Endings/Loss, Exorcism,

Wolfen Wicca 2
Class #9
Faery Trivia

Faery Trivia

The term Fairy (Faery) is rather an overall encompassing label of many many different beings. Under this term is a rather long list of being, but to give you an example we have Elves, Undines, Gnomes, Brownies, Deaves, Sprites, Leprechauns, and so on

Class #9
Faery Trivia page 2

When calling or talking about a Fairy you should always refer to them as, "Good Neighbor" or "Good People". The reason being that fairy means "malicious imp" its said that what you call or name them is how they will act. So better safe than sorry!

Mortal children have been exchanged down thru the centuries with fairy children. The fairies would replace the human child with one of theirs, taking the human child.. These mortal children that have been exchanged are called Changelings.

On a full Moon, find a fairy ring. Walk, run, dance 3 times deosil around the ring at exactly midnight. This will allow you to hear any fairies in the area and what they are saying.

"I walk two worlds, the Material and the Mystical, to me that is the natural order of things"

Wolfen Wicca 2
Class #9
The Four (4) Elements

© Lady Wolfen Mists 1992

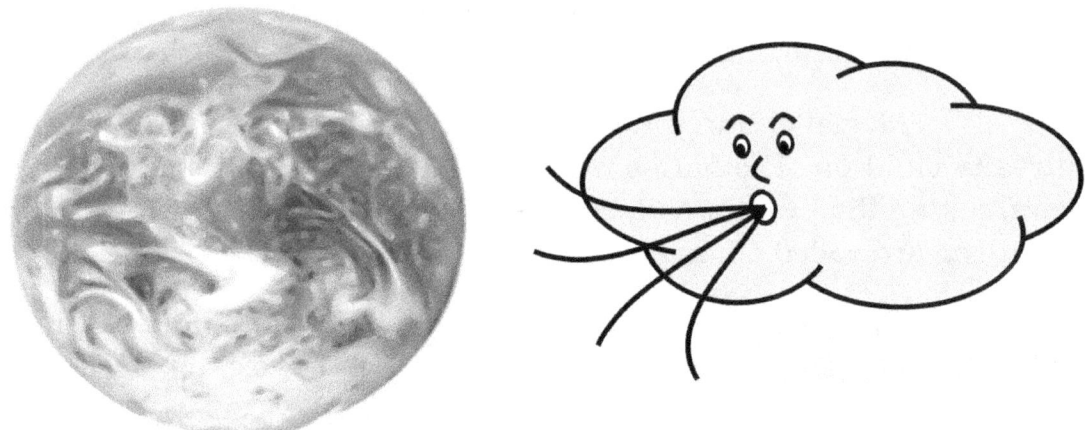

The Four (4)Directions, the Four (4) Elements, the Watchtowers, The Guardians there are many names that are used for the Four Corners of the Universe. Each corner or direction has a corresponding element. Each corresponding element has a specific power and area it covers. So when invoking a direction its important to know all one can about the direction you are dealing with.

The four basic elements are Fire, Water Air and Earth. These four elements are used to represent the Four states of being, from which everything we know and understand, is composed. This composition doesn't include only those qualities found on the Physical/Matter Plane of existence, but also the on the non-physical levels. This explains why we say: "So and so has a real fiery quality about her." What we are trying to say here is that even though So and so is human in the physical sense, there remains quality of fire about her on the non-physical reality. After all we aren't saying she is standing there in the physical form, burning like fire does! No instead we are saying that there is a part of them, on the non-physical realm, that contains the qualities of the element of Fire. When these qualities are displayed or allowed to rule, we conclude that the person in question has a fiery nature, and that Fire is a dominate part of this person spiritual make up.

Got it? Pretty easy isn't it. Yet a basic understanding of it is needed to successfully interact with the Universe. Some systems take the Four (4) Elements one step further and add a Fifth (5th) Element, that of Spirit. I personally like to use Spirit as a separate category in and of itself, it just seems natural to me. The Spirit or Ether category is seen as a perfect synthesis of all the elements together,

Wolfen Wicca 2; Our Walk Onward To Initiation

Class #9
The Four (4) Elements page 2

making an overall perfect guiding Spiritual Principle. As the Four (4) Elements make up what is seen as the physical/matter realm, Ether or Spirit makes up of the nonphysical, spiritual/emotional realm.

Lady Wolfen Mists

Wolfen Wicca 2
Class #9
Chart of the Elements

© Lady Wolfen Mists 1992

Element	Fire	Water	Air	Earth	Spirit
Quarter: & Color *represents*	South/ Red	West/Blue	East/ Yellow	North/Green	Center-Straight up-Iridescent White
Season: *represented*	Summer	Fall	Spring	Winter	All Year
Elementals: *Most common to exist here*	Salamanders & Dragons & Djinn's	Undines-Mermaids Mermen	Sylphs & Fairies who live in trees & flowers	Gnomes who live inside the earth	
Ruler here: *Who to call on to speak to those in charge of this place*	Djinn	Niksa (Undine)	Paralda (Sylphs)	Gob (Gnomes)	
Magickal Tool: *most commonly used to represent:*	Wand & Lamps, Red Candles	Chalice	Dagger & Incense	Pentacle & Salt	Incense & Secret Forces
Element	Fire	Water	Air	Earth	Spirit

Wolfen Wicca 2; Our Walk Onward To Initiation

Animal Totem: *Most common to this area, Master Level*	Lion	Eagle	Man	Bull	
Hour	Noon	Sunset	Sunrise	Midnight	
Symbol of	Individuality & Energy	Life & Never Ending Cycle	Mind & Creative Thoughts	Emotions & Strength Fertility	Eternal Soul & Interdependence of All
Tatter Symbol *Common Magickal system symbol:*	Red Triangle Point up	Silver Crescent	Blue Circle	Yellow Square	Black Oval

Wolfen Wicca 2
Class #9
Magickal Wells

Popular types of Magickal Wells

Wishing Wells- A special well where a friendly spirit dwells. This type of well is usually decorated with flowers and beautiful stones. People throw coins or items of value into the well, over their right shoulder, into the water in the well. The spirit in the well accepts the item and grants the wish. Wishing wells are very popular.

Holy Wells- These are wells that have a direct association with the Goddess or the Mother Image. The water contained herein this well is considered very sacred, holy and rejuvenation. There has usually been a vision of a Goddess appearing here, or there is a legend that this well had a specific part in the historically background of a specific Goddess.

Rag Wells- These type of wells are directly associated with healings. The people using the powers of this well usually leave bits of cloth tied to the surrounding trees and shrubs. These act as signals of the healing waters, and as token or gift to the spirit/deity who lives within the well. it is also seen as a celebration of the healing powers the well contains. The more personal or beautiful the cloth, the more pleasing it is to the spirit/deity.

Class #9
Magickal Wells Page 2

<u>Laughing Wells</u>- The waters that flow within these wells are bubbly and flowing, they contain a sparkle and effervesce. The natural springs are naturally carbonated. When doing divination with one of these wells one throws in a large object, the amount of bubbles released are then used to determine the answer to the inquiry.

Days of the Week & Their Significance

Day of Week	Ruling Planet	Magickal Properties
Sunday	Sun	Success, Fame Strength, Protection, Healing,
Monday	Moon	Peace, Psychic abilities, Purification, Compassion
Tuesday	Mars	Sex, Passions, Causes, Survival, Courage, Anger
Wednesday	Mercury	Divination, Wisdom, Travel, Spiritual Study
Thursday	Jupiter	Money, Prosperity, Success, Abundance, flow
Friday	Venus	Love, Beauty, Arts, Friendship. Renewal, Marriage
Saturday	Saturn	New Houses, Travel, Endings/Loss, Exorcism,

Wolfen Wicca 2
Samhain: An Overview of Traditions & Customs

© Lady Wolfen Mists 1992

Samhain is considered THE great Sabbat. It is said that a Witch may miss some of the festivals but none are t miss Samhain. It's been called many many names over the years. Names like, All Souls Night, Halloween, All Hallows Eve, Hallowmass. Samhain, Witches Night, Devils Night, Night of the Dead, just to mention a few. But no matter what one calls it or hears it called, none can deny that its roots are deeply bound to paganism. Samhain is the most Magickal night of the year. A powerful night when the worlds are closest and the magickal veils that separate us are thinnest they will ever be. As tradition dictates this festival begins at sundown on Oct.31st.

The Celts have much input into the traditional origin of Samhain. To begin with to the Celts Samhain meant the summers end. and marked the beginning of the New Year. Celtic history tells us that they divided the seasons of the year into two (2) sections. The first section ran from Beltane to Samhain, being the summer section. The second section ran from Samhain to Beltane, being the winter section. By todays calendar we divide the year into four (4) distinct sections. Placing samhain at the beginning of winter and the end of autumn.

The pronunciation of samhain varies as to the language you are referring to. In Gaelic its pronounced *Sow-In*. The Scots say *Sav-en*. But the USA has the most untraditional pronunciation of all. they say *Sam-hane,* personally this particular pronunciation drives me nuts! I much prefer the more traditional ways of saying Samhain, but its up to you as to what pronunciation you feel more comfortable with.

Yet no matter how you pronounce this festival there are two main concepts that can be seen woven throughout. They are the celebration of the ancestors, or feast of the dead, and divination.

Wolfen Wicca 2; Our Walk Onward To Initiation

Samhain: An Overview of Traditions & Customs
Page 2

There are other traditions that also see this night as a very sacred and powerful day. For example the Egyptians celebrated this night as the festival of the Dead, as did the Mayans and many ancient Mexican traditions.

It is believed that on this one night, when the veils lift, the dead can rise. If they wish to return to the Earth plane then they can pass through the open portals at will. Torches are set out to guide them home as well as candles being burnt. Incense are lit to entice the departed to visit. Food is set aside for them as well as place settings being set at tables awaiting their arrival. Dancing and singing are a major part of this festival. Altars to the ancestors are set up on this night to honor those souls who have crossed over. But all the entities must return to their world, and the veils close again by the time the cock-crows in the morning.

Concerning the second concept of Divination and fortune telling, there is no other time considered as receptive to telling the future as this time. There are many different types of divination going on this night, everything from the traditional tarot cards, tea leaf reading to scrying in a crystal ball. As well as the more uncommon methods of fortune telling like, cutting an apple in half crosswise, so the pentagram shows inside. Then eat the apple while looking into a mirror, asking out loud who will be your future spouse. Then looking over your shoulder into the mirror you should be able to see the face of your spouse. Another scrying technique that is used to tell the future at this particular time is candle wax drippings. Almost any type of divination on this night is sure to get successful answers.

But now you may be wondering about all the accouterments that come with Samhain. Like the use of Jack O lanterns. It's thought that these lanterns were originally made from gourds and not pumpkins, and were another Celtic custom. The lanterns were traditionally cut into scary faces with candles put inside to scare off any negative spirits traveling by and protect the user of the jack o lantern. They were also placed out porches as a form of protection for the home. Bobbing for apples has another interesting history. Its thought to be the last bits of a rite referred to as "seining", which is somewhat like a Christian baptism. The rite was said to involve the Cauldron of Regeneration. The inductees head was placed over the cauldron and water was poured over it. Then after a series of questions were asked and answered the inductees head was completely immersed in the liquid within the cauldron. The hands of the inductee were tied, usually behind the back, and the eyes were blindfolded. This same theme is seen in the game bobbing for apples. In this traditional party game the participant bends over a tub (cauldron) of water, in which sacred life giving fruit is floating. The participant must catch the apple in their mouth (like feeding the spirit), and while trying to achieve this feat they usually immerse their heads in the water (a symbol of rebirth). Their hands are usually behind their backs, they can be tied, and they can be or not be blindfolded.

Samhain: An Overview of Traditions & Customs
Page 3

      Lastly lets look at the custom of "trick or treating". It also is thought to be Celtic in origin. But in actuality it was more for the adults then the children. The adults would often wear costumes, usually reverse role dress. Men as Women and Women as Men honoring the energies within each other. Then once the costumes were put on they then went from door to door seeking treats. the adult "treats" were usually alcoholic in nature or sweet-meats. Wassail bowls were found in almost all the homes visited. As well as seasonal songs being sung from one house to another, much like caroling today.

      So when Samhain approaches this year think back on these traditions/customs. Maybe you might even want to see how many "ties" to the old ways you can recognize in the many public celebrations held here. But most of all, at this time of the year, remember to Honor your ancestors and look forward to the bright New Years to come!

Bright Blessings to all
Lady Wolfen Mists

"Looking to the New Year as the Great Wheel turns"

Wolfen Wicca 2
Class #9
Samhain Sabbat Group Version

© Lady Wolfen Mists 1991

The altar is set up in the usual manner with the exception of a black candle in the center of the white and red ones. This ritual is set up for a group activity but can easily be written (interpreted) for solitary. The circle is cast ahead of time. There is also a stand in the center of the circle of the cauldron to be placed upon. You should dress in a festive manner, wearing all your magickal jewelry. it is at this time, initiates may wear your sword, dagger or other weapon.

All come to the edge of the circle :

Circle Caster:
"Who comes to my circle?"

All Say: "We come to celebrate Samhain"

Circle Caster;
"How do you come?"

All Say; "In Perfect Love and Perfect Trust"

Circle Caster says:
(while cutting an opening)
"Then enter in Perfect Love and Perfect Trust."

All file in, the High Priestess and High Priest take their positions at the altar. The High Priestess lights the red candle and says;

High Priestess:
"Welcome Samhain! I light this candle to call the horned One, so he may celebrate this sabbat with us in our circle. (*lights red candle with taper*)

High Priest:
"Welcome Samhain! On this night when the veils are thin and great bonfires are lit. We ask the Bright Lady to join us in our celebration of the Samhain Sabbat." (*High Priest lights the white candle with the taper*)

High Priest/ess together light the black candle

High Priestess;
"It is at this time we celebrate the ancestors who have passed on and the renewal of the soul. The renewal of life taken from the Bright Lady's Cauldron of regeneration. It seems appropriate that this be our Witches New Year!

Samhain Sabbat Group Version Page 2

All Say
"Hail to the New Year!"

High Priest ;
"Hail to coming of the Crone and the aged Sage

High Priestess picks up the Cauldron that is decorated with fall items, oak leafs and acorn. She reaches inside the cauldron and pulls out the crones black veils, puts them on.

High Priestess;
" In the days of old it was tradition that fall would ritually burn those things that were undesirable, purifying themselves for the new year to come each of you has brought to the circle those things you would like to put at rest this year. Place those pieces of paper into the cauldron as I pass before you."

High Priest;
"In the days of old it was custom to dance around the bonfires after burning those things one wished to put to rest.   Tonight I will follow, as a representative of the Horned One, and Purify you with the incense I carry. I ask that you turn three times clockwise in the smoke of the incense."

After all have dropped their papers into the cauldron and all have been purified, then the High Priest/ess, return to the front of the altar. The High Priestess returns the incense to the altar. The High Priest sets the cauldron on the table set up for this purpose.

High Priest (*as he lights the papers***)**
"My time grows short, your ashes go with me to the underworld. There they will stay. The Battle of the brothers begins, the Oak and Holly Lords fight for position. Even now my power fades, my leafs fall, my sap dries any bones begin to snap. The cycle of death is upon me, regeneration nears. I escort the Crone to the Underworld with me, we rest and await the cycle to turn once more."

High Priestess;
In this time out of time, In this place out of place, on a day that is not. In a place between worlds and planes. In this sacred temple of the Ancient Ones. We play out the drama of life and death. Hear me well children, as I leave you at this time to rest. Fear not the dark months that surround you. Know that I shall return to you. In only a few months Our Lord will be reborn and the cycle will begin again as it is meant to be."

Wolfen Wicca 2; Our Walk Onward To Initiation

Samhain Sabbat Group Version Page 3

High Priest;
"My Lady, we must not tarry to long, for even now I feel my brothers pulse waiting to enter. I see him at the circles edge full of power and life. Let us go!"

At the edge of the circle "runs" the Holly Lord, waiting with much eagerness to come into the circle. The Oak Lord, tired and sore holds the cauldron, and reaches for the Crones hand. They both walk three times around the circle in a deosil fashion. Each time they pass the members, the members bow and may speak openly to them. After the third pass they both stand before the South Gate. The Circle Caster opens the circle for them to pass through, while they pass all say;

All Say;
" Fare thee well Oak Lord and grandmother Crone, till we meet again may your rest be peaceful. Merry Part! Blessed Be!

The Circle Caster closes the south gate. All heads are bowed for 13 heartbeats, while all think on what has gone on this night. At this time the High Priest and High Priestess return to join the circle, They stand with the other members of the Grove.
At the edge of the circle at the East gate, a flute is heard. All look towards the East gate. There stands the Holly Lord. The circle caster rushes to the gate.

Circle Caster;*(circle caster allows them entrance)*
"Who now comes to our circle dressed in Holly?"

Holly Lord;
"I come to your circle, The Holly Lord. It is my time now. I enter children in perfect Love and Perfect Trust."

Circle Caster; *Circle Caster opens the East gate and bows down saying;*
"All hail the Holly Lord, here to see us through the Dark season!"

All Say;
"Welcome Holly Lord! Welcome! Welcome!"

Holly Lord *(standing in front of the altar)*
"On this night of Samhain, the flames of the material world glow and all that was is no longer. Tonight, my brother the Oaken Lord and Crone go to rest in the underworld. Their spirits shall burn forever in worlds beyond, and they shall return when the time is right. For now it is I who will remind you of life, with my Green Holly Leafs. It is I who shall sustain you through these cold dark days. It is

Samhain Sabbat Group Version Page 4

through the wisdom of the Crone and the passions of the Mother and the glory and innocence of the maiden that all things continue. There is truly no death only rest and rebirth for all, for this is one of the Great Mysteries of the Ancients.

You as followers of the ancients must hold no fear. You must have an understanding of the Never Ending Cycle. You must understand the different aspects of the Goddess and God and how they fit into your lives. It is sometimes true that not all in life is fair, that for some spring lasts longer than others. Yet, even in the failing of the Oak and Crone, there is much to learn of those aspects. perhaps you, who feel cheated, did not need so long to learn the secrets of the ages and your wisdom is now in its full bloom. I warn you not to waste even a single day in pity that your reign in an aspect may be to short. It is as it was meant to be. Learn all that you can and Love with all your heart. For these things, learning and loving are the center of all things. Worry not at the amount of time you are given for you shall   never truly end. The never-ending cycle of life, death, rebirth shall continue always. It is the rhythm of the   Universe. Those you love now will never stop loving. This is the word of the Threefold Goddess and Her Consort, the Lord of Light. May all that hear it open their heart and truly receive its meaning. So mote it be!"

All Say; "So mote it be!"

Holly Lord:
"Now let the revels begin! May our New Year be a happy and prosperous one."

If there are cakes and wine, this is the time to do that. Start from the blessing of the cakes and wine. The circle can now be opened for anyone to say or do anything they like. Once this is finished all have participated who wished to, the circle caster banishes the circle as usual.
Because this is done inside in a small area, we must banish the circle before t he feasting and entertainment. If we were outside or even in a bigger area, all this would continue to go on inside the circle.

Invocation of Talisen

Talisen is an aspect of the God who is the Creative Thought. The inspiration put to paper, the idea in the mind. Tonight would be a wonderful time to invoke his creative energies, especially if you are solitary. We have done this in a group before and have had wonderful success. Everything from finishing a story to creating music to painting have happened this invocation. One of the ones I like best is a friend who had been have much much difficultly with a computer

Wolfen Wicca 2; Our Walk Onward To Initiation

Samhain Sabbat Group Version Page 5

program he had been writing. He had spent hours trying to figure out what was wrong, debugging it and then doing it again and again. He had almost given up. He brought this problem to the circle when Talisen was invoked and within 15 minutes he had figured out what was wrong, and within 30 minutes he had the whole thing rewritten, debugged and working! Now that's power!!!! So if you'd like to try heres the invocation we use.

******If time permits Talisen can be invoked. Do this right <u>after the circle is opened to all</u>, allow the members to talk, then close the circle. *******

Raise up your dominate hand. All walk around the circle in a deosil fashion
say the following:

High Priestess;

" I invoke and call to my circle the facet of the god known as Talisen. It is his male energies I seek. Come Talisen and fill me, bring your creative forces into my sacred space and into me. Rain those energies into the air that I may breath them and become one with you. Make them strong and sure so that I may feel your creative force pulsing through my veins. Pushing me to create and succeed and to be confident in myself and my creations."

When you feel the tingle in the air and sense His presence,

High Priestess says:

"Welcome Talisen, I am but an empty vessel to be filled with your positive guidance and creative energies. Welcome now!"

Next all settle down and allow the creative process to begin. Once all are finished with their creative work the circle is banished in the usual manner. With the exception of thanking the God Talisen for his coming and his inspiration. All energies are told to return to their respective homes until we next meet.

Wolfen Wicca 2
Class #9
Samhain Sabbat- Solitary Version

© Lady Wolfen Mists 1991

The altar is set up in the usual manner with the exception of a black candle in the center of the white and red ones. The circle is cast ahead of time. There is also a stand in the center of the circle of the cauldron to be placed upon. You should dress in a festive manner, wearing all your magickal jewelry. it is at this time, initiates may wear your sword, dagger or other weapon.

At the edge of the circle :
Say:
"I have cast the circle to celebrate Samhain. In Perfect Love and Perfect Trust"

Take your position in front of the altar and light the red candle and says;

Say:
"Welcome Samhain! I light this candle to call the horned One, so he may celebrate this sabbat with me in our circle. (*lights red candle with taper*)
"Welcome Samhain! On this night when the veils are thin and great bonfires are lit. We ask the Bright Lady to join in the celebration of the Samhain Sabbat." (*lights the white candle with the taper*)

Wait 13 heart beats and *light the black candle*

Say
"It is at this time we celebrate the ancestors who have passed on and the renewal of the soul. The renewal of life taken from the Bright Lady's Cauldron of regeneration. It seems appropriate that this be our Witches New Year!

Wait 3 heartbeats

Say;
"Hail to coming of the Crone and the aged Sage,

Pick up the Cauldron that is decorated with fall items, oak leafs and acorn. Reaches inside the cauldron and pulls out the crones black veils, puts them on.

Say;
" In the days of old it was tradition that fall would ritually burn those things that were undesirable, purifying themselves for the new year to come I have brought to the circle those things I would like to put at rest this year. Written in signs and symbols that I understand.

Place those pieces of paper into the cauldron

Wolfen Wicca 2; Our Walk Onward To Initiation

Samhain Sabbat- Solitary Version Page 2

Wait 3 heart beats

Say;
"In the days of old it was custom to dance around the bonfires after burning those things one wished to put to rest. Tonight I will follow, as a representative of the Horned One, and Purify myself with the incense.

Now turn three times clockwise in the smoke of the incense. When completed return to the front of the altar, put the incense to the altar. Place the cauldron on the table set up for this purpose.

Say (*as he lights the papers*)
"The time of the Oak Lord grows short, your ashes go with me to the underworld. There they will stay. The Battle of the brothers begins, the Oak and Holly Lords fight for position. Even now my power fades, my leafs fall, my sap dries any bones begin to snap. The cycle of death is upon me, regeneration nears. I escort the Crone to the Underworld with me, we rest and await the cycle to turn once more."

Wait 1 3 heartbeats,

Say;
"In this time out of time, In this place out of place, on a day that is not. In a place between worlds and planes. In this sacred temple of the Ancient Ones. We play out the drama of life and death. Know well, as I, your Crone Mother, leave you at this time to rest. Fear not the dark months that surround you. Know that I shall return to you. In only a few months Our Lord will be reborn and the cycle will begin again as it is meant to be."

Meditate on the Oak Lord and Crone for a few minutes, see them leaving by the south gate.

Say;
"Fare thee well Oak Lord and Grandmother Crone, till we meet again may your rest be peaceful. Merry Part! Blessed Be!

Now meditate on the east gate, listen and see in your minds eye. At the edge of the circle at the East gate, a flute is heard. All look towards the East gate. There stands the holly Lord. You rush to the gate.

Say;
"All hail the Holly Lord, here to see us through the Dark season "Welcome Holly Lord! Welcome! Welcome!" Now let the revels begin! May our New Year be a happy and prosperous one."

Lady Wolfen Mists

Samhain Sabbat- Solitary Version Page 3

If there are cakes and wine, this is the time to do that. Start from the blessing of the cakes and wine, allow open circle time to do what you want (invocation of Talisen here).Once you are finished banish the circle as usual.

Invocation of Talisen

Talisen is an aspect of the God who is the Creative Thought. The inspiration put to paper, the idea in the mind. Tonight would be a wonderful time to invoke his creative energies, especially if you are solitary. We have done this in a group before and have had wonderful success. Everything from finishing a story to creating music to painting have happened this invocation. One of the ones I like best is a friend who had been have much much difficultly with a computer program he had been writing. He had spent hours trying to figure out what was wrong, debugging it and then doing it again and again. He had almost given up. He brought this problem to the circle when Talisen was invoked and within 15 minutes he had figured out what was

wrong, and within 30 minutes he had the whole thing rewritten, debugged and working! Now that's power!!!! So if you'd like to try here's the invocation we use.

*******If time permits Talisen can be invoked. Do this right <u>after the circle is opened to all</u>, allow the members to talk, then close the circle.*

Raise up your dominate hand. All walk around the circle in a deosil fashion say the following:

High Priestess;

" I invoke and call to my circle the facet of the God known as Talisen. It is his male energies I seek. Come Talisen and fill me, bring your creative forces into my sacred space and into me. Rain those energies into the air that I may breath them and become one with you. Make them strong and sure so that I may feel your creative force pulsing through my veins. Pushing me to create and succeed and to be confident in myself and my creations.

When you feel the tingle in the air and sense His presence, **Say:**

"Welcome Talisen, I am but an empty vessel to be filled with your positive guidance and creative energies. Welcome now!"

Next all settle down and allow the creative process to begin. Once you are finished the circle is banished in the usual manner. With the exception of thanking the God Talisen for his coming and his inspiration. All energies are told to return to their respective homes until we next meet.

Wolfen Wicca 2
Class #9
Practical Instructions

© Lady Wolfen Mists 1991

Do a solitary circle Casting and Invoke Talisen. Use the ritual included as a guide, it is for a group but you can convert it to solitary. Report what you were inspired to create during this time. What did the Circle feel like at this time? How did you feel? This will be reviewed when you submit your work for Initiation ☺

"Alone but still with my pack...The Universe"

Notes on Invocation Of Talisen

Notes on Class 9

Lady Wolfen Mists

Wolfen Wicca 2
Class #10

© Lady Wolfen Mists Jan.1990
revised 2001

Theory:
    Auras --The Three (3) levels
    Auras --How to See them
    Color & Color Treatment
    Music & its effect on Auras
    Aura Recording body chart
    Tracker Wolf Oil Recipe
    Tracker Wolf Pathwork

Practical:
    Use the Tracker Wolf Pathwork

Circle Work:
    What is your inspirational thought for the week.

***Assignment: *** **Students in your Magickal Journal:**
Do the Tracker Wolf Pathwork and tell me all about it, How did it go? What wolf did you use? What did you find out? This will be reviewed when you submit your work for Initiation ☺

"I Walk On!

Wolfen Wicca 2
Class #10
Auras: 3 Basic Levels

© Lady Wolfen Mists 1992

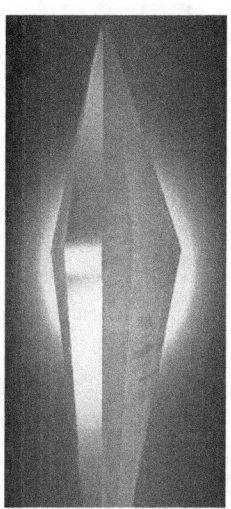

Auras, that mystical word that seems to be passed around a lot these days. Everybody has one, they can be "seen" by the trained eye, photographed by the right kind of camera, they can even be felt! But what are they????

To explain the Aura that surrounds all living things you must first understand the idea of the body and cell structure. The human body consists of cells that vibrate (oscillate) constantly, this oscillation varies for each being and sets up that persons own vibratory rate. Got that? Ok, now with that in mind lets move forward with that same idea. Each and every vibratory rate, per whole person, is programmed by that persons DNA. Thus no two vibratory rates can ever be exactly the same, there will always be some differences, no matter how small. Vibratory rates are as individual as DNA. So the cell, which contains the DNA, can only transmit and receive these distinctive frequencies. Thus the body itself establishes its own unique vibratory rate.

Next the vibratory rate in turn establishes an Electromagnetic Field, which can be measured by scientific electronic instruments. This Electromagnetic field is what is commonly called the AURA. One of the instruments that can be used to establish the existence of the Auraic field is Kirilian Photography. In this type of photography a limited amount of radiation is introduced into the vibrational field and the result is a photo that looks "ghostly". It shows a outline of the image which is surrounded by various colors at various densities, this is the vibratory/auric field of the subject. It is that field, which is found surrounding all living things, which is called an Aura.

Class #10
Auras: 3 Basic Levels Page 2

3 Basic Levels in a Aura

Its said that the aura can be broken down into at least 3 distinctive levels, each acting on its own and interacting with the other levels. The first two levels combine to make the final one. For the beginner who is training to "see" auras the final level will be enough. Yet it is after you have worked at seeing auras and read enough to have a reference point you will begin to notice all the color changes at all the distinctive levels.

Now lets look at a breakdown of all three levels and a little about them:

1) **Your Inner Aura (closest to your skin)**
This is the direct power of Light and Life. It come to you directly from the God and Goddess. It is here that your level of energy is established. This level of the aura creates a "Goddess and God Center", that establishes your level of Spiritual commitment. It is also this level that determines how you are in the physical (subconscious) aspect.

2) **Your Middle Aura (center)**
This area interacts and reports mainly what is going on in the emotional levels of your being. It is here that you find the center of responses (conscious level) to the world around you and the environmental stimuli present. Many "readers" use this level as an indicator of the level of stress in the individuals life and how well they are coping with that stress.

3) **Your Final Aura Level (furthest away from the skin, the outside)**
This level is constantly changing depending on the reactions of the first two levels. It is a combination of how you combine the spiritual and the physical, in the everyday work and in common situations. It is a general holistic view/picture of the first two levels, and should be seen as such. If there are areas of concern, it is recommended that a more in depth reading take place at the appropriate level, so that the cause can be established. Once the cause has been located, as to which level, then the individual is directed to work on that specific problem and that overall level of existence.

So there you have it, a very quick look at the Aura and its 3 basic levels. In closing of this section I would like to give you this last bit of information concerning the aura. I found it interesting, but wasn't sure where to put it, so I'll put it here. The Aura itself, is a part of the overall body, in that it is with you and your body from the time you are born until the time you cross. But as much as it is part of the body it is also apart from the body, existing on a non physical level, giving us a non-physical reflection of who we are. An example of this is if you lose

Class #10
Auras: 3 Basic Levels Page 3

a part of your physical body, say a leg. When your aura is felt, viewed or photographed the missing leg will still be included in the overall aura! The physical missing leg is still a part of other non-physical body, and still registers as such, and belongs to you.

Lady Wolfen Mists

Wolfen Wicca 2
Class #10
Steps to Getting in Touch with your Aura
(How to see others)

© Lady Wolfen Mists 1992

1. Use a White background to see the aura. Some people say to use a beige or black background. I have tried all of these, and although it works, I have had better (easier) success with the white background.

2. Next find a living thing, a plant or a person works well, which you can put of the background and focus on. I suggest that you use your own hand in the beginning, against white paper. If you wear glasses it may help you to remove them.

3. Focus your eyes just past the physical edge of the item your using, in this case your hand. Allow your eyes to "fixate or get stuck " here. Become aware of the light that is emanating from the very edge of your hand. It may be <u>very</u> thin without much color to start with. But that light surrounding the item is your electro-magnetic. field, YOUR AURA! For those of you who know how to "Magic Eye" where the 3 dimensional picture pops up at you from some geometric design, allow your eyes to do the same here. Now that you can do it, practice until you can see color fluctuations or even a combination of colors.

4. For those of you still having problems try this next exercise. This exercise has been <u>very successful</u> with students, in the past, to train their eyes to see/recognise auras.

(a). Place both index fingers pointing towards each other, in front of your eyes. About nose/eyes level. Don't let the finger tips touch. You will see both fingers with fingertips pointing at each other, and a small **"finger-like football"** between those pointing finger tips.

Steps to Getting in Touch with your Aura
(How to see others) Page 2

(b). It is the middle "finger football"" that I want you to focus your attention on. Become aware of it. Notice the blurry edges the lighter "shadow like" levels that surround it. Become aware of the colors, the fluctuations in size/color levels. That's your Aura!

5. Don't take time to analyze the information you are seeing, just allow it to flow, take in what you see. If you follow the above steps and practice, you should be able to train your eyes, to see the auras of all living thing in no time.

Wolfen Wicca 2
Class #10
Colors & Color Treatments

© Lady Wolfen Mists 1992

There are many times when we would like to get a certain attribute more balanced or energized within ourselves and our lives. When the Harmony inside just cant seem to be balanced no matter what you do. That's the perfect time to try a color treatment for your aura. First determine using your intuition and an Aura reading what level of the aura is the problem stemming from. Next check with the color chart as to the corresponding color for your particular problem.

There are many different ways to use color to help the aura and give treatments. I will only mention two that I like, they are easy so beginners can do them with no problems, and are quite effective. In both techniques you need to be sprayed lightly or sponged with warm water. This is to open the Auric field and adjust the vibratory level to the particular colors level, so the color and energies may be successfully and totally infused in to the aura as needed.

The first technique is OK, but not my favorite. Make, buy or sew cloth sheets of each color long enough to cover the entire body. Put the sheet on the person and lay there for the allotted amount of time. You may have some trouble covering the hear area with this technique.

The second one is much better and seems to work well for me. Get colored light bulbs, or if you cant find them take color cellophane and make "slides" to be used with a white light bulb, If you can find full spectrum bulbs that's even better! Turn on the light bulb and place the colored cellophane slide under it so the light passes through the cellophane and the colored of the slide is emitted.

Class #10
Colors & Color Treatments Page 2

(**CAUTION**: Be sure to be careful when using this technique. Always have someone there who is watching the heat levels, the slides can get to warm and may catch fire if let go to long) Now dressed or undressed (which ever way you feel most comfortable) lay down under the colors. Allow the colors to pour over you for a particular amount of time. Crystals, stones or even music can be added here to combine energies to the over all effect.

Lastly in both techniques be sure to rinse with cool water when done. This is to close the Auric field completely, and position the new energies as needed.

Crystal can be used by both the person whose aura is being read, and the person who is doing the reading. The crystal is used to enhance the colors, making them more visible to the naked eye. All you need to do is to get, find or buy a Generator Crystal and program it for use with auras. Then either the reader, or the person being read, can hold it while the reading is being done. When finished with the crystal be sure to rinse with cool water, not tap, as it contains many funky minerals and such. I use distilled or spring water if possible, Then lay the crystal in the window to get sun or moon light to repower the natural energies contained inside the crystal itself. Leave in the light for approx. 2 hours once the crystal has become to dirty to work with, or is need of fresh energies

Wolfen Wicca 2
Class #10
Music & the Aura

© Lady Wolfen Mists Jan.1990
revised 2001

The aura is affected by everything around you, but especially by emotion. Music often evokes very strong feeling in many of us, this is reflected in our auras. It can be seen by the "trained eye". Sharps are said to intensify a color, while Flats combine colors into dazzling combinations. Below is a chart that lists the color, the corresponding note and the area that is affected within the human being.

AURA - MUSIC CHART

These are the known affects of musical note upon the human Auraic Field

Color	Note	Area Affected
RED	C	The Physical Self
ORANGE	D	Mental & Physical
YELLOW	E	Learning & Social Contacts
GREEN	F	Healing & Visualization
BLUE	G	Balance in All Things
VIOLET	B/A	Higher Spiritual Self, Creativity

Wolfen Wicca 2
Class #10

© Lady Wolfen Mists Jan. 1990
revised 2001

Color Use, Meaning & Color Treatment for Auras

Colors	Description:	Time:
Red	Sexuality, Passion, Physical, Need to have end results, Intensity	25-30 minutes
Yellow	Vitality, Oneness, learning, Higher Intelligence, positive outlook	25-30 minutes
Orange	Rapid Mental Energy, quick wit & Good sense of Humor Planned Life & actions, Strong Will	25-30 minutes
Green	Growth Healing & Massage energies often used in Mental emotional & physical healing/counseling	25-30 minutes
Violet	The Arcane Arts, Higher Intuitive Powers, Psychic, Finding Higher self Supreme Balance & Harmony with Universe	25-30 minutes
White	All colors combined in the Universal Balance, Unconditional Love & Understanding, Acceptance, "God/dess Light"	30-35 minutes
Blue	Peace, Balance, Harmony Truth, Healing, Creativity	10-15 minutes

Blue must not exceed 15 minutes & should be followed by 15 minutes of red . Any more than 15 minutes of Blue and you turn into a mellowed out doormat!

Wolfen Wicca 2
Class 10
Aura Recording Body Chart

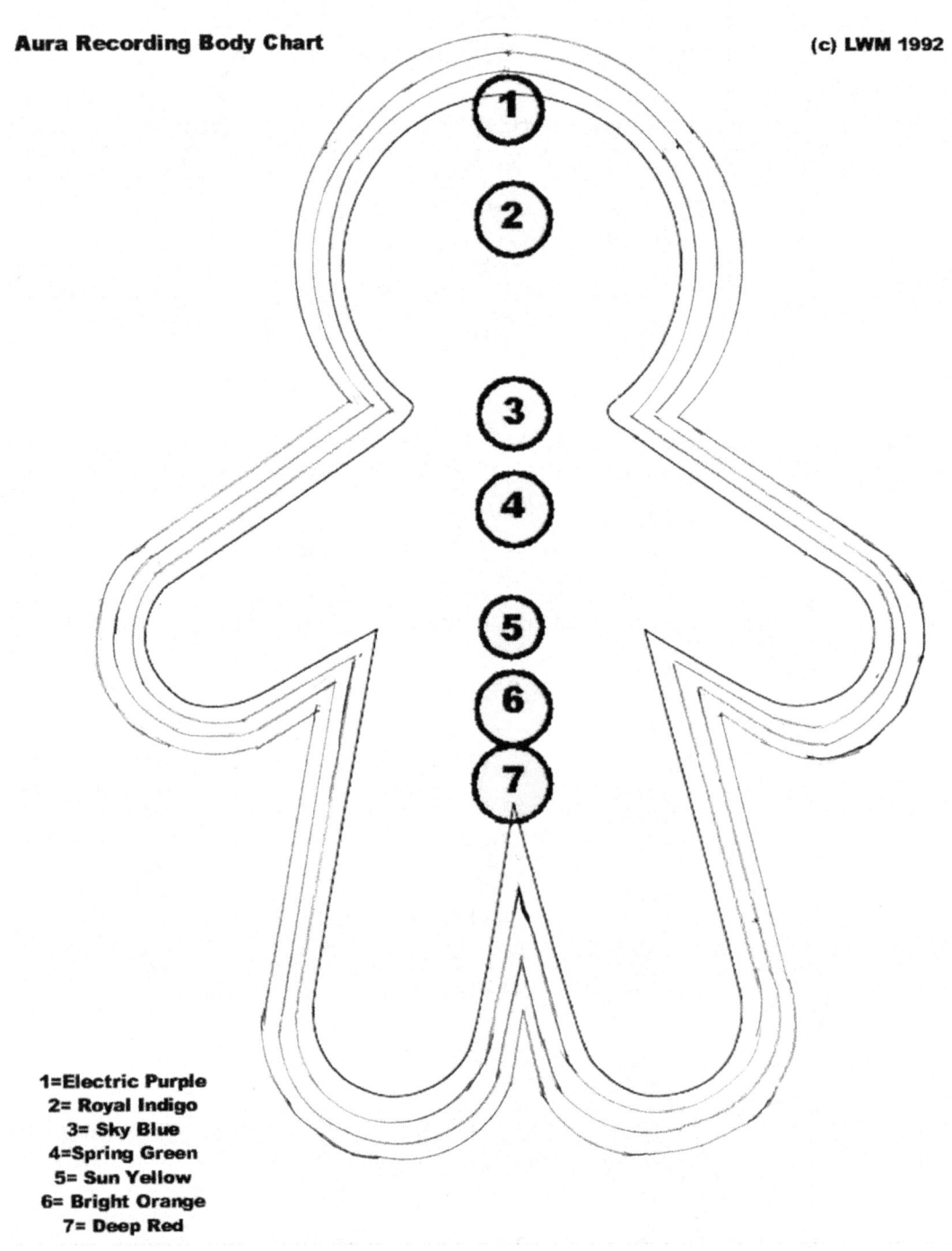

Wolfen Wicca 2
Class #10
Tracker Wolf Oil Recipe

© Lady Wolfen Mists Jan.1992

Tracker Wolf Oil Recipe

Mix 50ml of Grapeseed oil

- 15 drops of Sweet Oil
- 20 drops of Ambergris Oil
- 3 drops of Lime Oil
- 2 drops of Cajeput oil

Mix well in a deosil fashion, and let sit for 3-6 hours. When Mixing in your minds eye Visualize all Tracker Wolves working for your Highest Good on the astral and bringing to you that which you request.

Wolfen Wicca 2
Class #10
Tracker Wolf Pathworking

© Lady Wolfen Mists Jan. 1992

This is a Pathworking that you can do to send out you tracker wolf to "see" whats going on. You can use it for many things, like sending it out to see if someone or something is sending negative energies to you and causing you harm. Another example is to check on someone you care about to make sure they are safe from the hexes or curses of another. Tracker Wolf works on the astral plane but can "see" into many planes of existence. What ever reason you wish Tracker Wolf to do, you MUST have a symbol of what you think this particular wolf would look like. It can be a drawing or something you found on the inter net or pictures from a calendar or magazine. In any case you get the drift, each Tacker you want to use must have an assigned task, In example you want to check on your Lover and see if they are telling you the truth, you would pick out a wolf that would represent Sexy wolf. You would keep that picture and use it only for that task, so each task the wolf does you must have a symbol for to help you visualize what your wolf would look like.

To begin with you will need to cast and entire circle with the usual altar set up, you don't need to light the candles as you will be deeply meditating and visualizing. Take the picture of the wolf you have chosen to represent the facet of the Tracker Wolf you will be using. Place it on the altar and focus your energies on it and what the task you want Tracker Wolf to preform for you. Next anoint your 3rd eye with a small drop of Tracker Wolf Oil.

Class #10
Tracker Wolf Pathworking Page 2

Sit down or lay down in the circle and go to your safe place. Once there call your wolf to you, you may ask its name so you can call it in the future. Say something like this when you call it to you.

> "Silent night in a star filled Sky.
> Send this Tracker Wolf to my side.
> Let it gather the information I need
> In this Tracker I give you the lead
>
> Protecting me from all that has gone wrong,
> Alerting me with its wolf song.
> Tracker Wolf on ALL levels go,
> All that may hurt me I want you to show
>
> So Mote It Be!"

Once the wolf comes to you (you will see/feel it in your minds eye) speak with it and explain in full the task you would like it to do and why. Remember it will only act for your Highest good so only positive things here.

Visualize everything you say to the wolf with the deepest amount of detail you can, this may take a few moments. Now send it out of your safe place to preform the task for you. Telling it that you will either meet it here in the circle again in 24 hours or it can tell you the information it gathers in your dreams. Personally I like the dreams as the information for me is stronger there and clearer, but I warn you this all takes time and PRACTICE. So if it doesn't work 100% at first just keep trying until it flows easily.

Now all that's left to do is banish your circle and clean up. Be sure to place your wolf picture in a safe place until you need it again for this type of task, you can write the name of this wolf on the back of the picture.

(Optional) If you don't want to use the Tracker Oil you can carry the following bag to become open to the positive energies and call your wolf to your side. The size of the stones really don't matter, its how they feel in your hand. They should warm quickly and pulse as you hold them.

One small bag (cloth or leather)
Hematite
Petrified Wood
Fluorite
salt (just a pinch)

Wolfen Wicca 2
Class #10
Practical; Wolf Tracker Pathworking

© Lady Wolfen Mists Jan.1992
revised 2015

Instructions to the Practical Section

Do the Tracker Wolf Pathwork and tell me all about it, How did it go? What wolf did you use? What did you find out?

Notes on Class 10

Wolfen Wicca 2
Our Walk Onward To Initiation
Class #11

© Lady Wolfen Mists Jan.1990
revised 2001

Theory:
  Drawing Down the Moon
  Positions Drawing Down the Moon
  Drawing Down Ritual
  Charge
  Sabbat Info.
  Where to place the altar
  Triple Goddess potpourri recipe
  Myth of the Goddess

Circle Work:
What is your inspirational thought for the week.

Practical:
  Circle Cast
  Mock walk through on Drawing Down the Moon

***Assignment: <u>**Students in your Magickal Journal**</u>:
  Tell me how your Drawing Down the Moon went.
This will be reviewed when you submit your work for Initiation ☺

"I Walk On!

Wolfen Wicca 2
Class #11
Information on Drawing Down the Moon

© Lady Wolfen Mists 1992 revised 2000

General Information

Drawing Down The Moon is very traditional rite that is used to call the actual presence of the Goddess into the body of the High Priestess. The Goddess is called down to merge into the body of a selected female, usually the High Priestess, so that she may instruct and share with the members of the grove Her loving wisdom. Her actual presence through the body of the High Priestess adds immeasurably to the power generated in the circle. Yet so there is no misunderstanding in the actual "merging" of the Goddess into the body, we need to explain Inspiration verses. Possession.

First there is the act of **_Inspiration_**, which is what is done in this rite. The High Priest reads what is known as The Charge, which calls the Goddess down, then the High Priestess asks that the Goddess use her to speak and teach the grove (coven). The Goddess then enters the High Priestess and fills her mind , using her physical body as a vessel for the words and works that the Goddess chooses to share this night. It also needs to be understood here that the High Priestess **_retains all control of her own body, mind and actions. Most women explain it as "simply moving over as the Goddess inspires them to say or do what ever She wishes them to do."_** The memory of the High Priestess usually remains intact here with some bits and pieces missing, meaning that the High Priestess can usually remember what was said or done.

What is Possession if the above is Inspiration?

The act of possession, which is not part of Wicca, is an act that the person asks that the spirit of the entity in question, come into their body and take over. The spirit takes <u>complete control of the physical body</u> and the person

Class #11
Information on Drawing Down the Moon page 2

moves out or away from their own physical body. This moving out allows the spirit complete and total control of the person on all levels of existence. When this happens the memory of the person whose body is being possessed is usually very clouded, or recall is just not available at all. One of the religions that uses possession is Santeria. A particular God or Goddess is asked to possess a body and work through that body. The persons walk, speech and movement all take on the characteristics of that God/dess possessing the body. Some people even report that there are physical changes that take place in the possession, like the face changing to look like the God/dess possessing the person, all this ends and the body returns to normal when the God/dess completes their work and returns to the non-physical realm. The body is released and returns to its normal functioning/look.

We in Wicca do not participate in Possession as it takes away free will (and taking away free will breaks the harm ye none.) Instead we allow for the inspiration of the God/dess to flow over us and allow their words and ideas to be shared with others in the coven/grove. This is a very electric time and very sacred. You can almost feel their presence and reach out to touch them . I have had special messages for individuals that brought them to tears of happiness as well as loving comments that in my normal life I had no idea that the person was in need. The God/dess speaks from my heart to them in calling down the moon and allows for much guidance for us as a group and individuals.

Can you do Calling down the Moon Solitary?

Of course you can, its nice to have balanced polarities within the circle (male and female energies) But its not necessary. You need only call the Goddess down into yourself, (assume the positions needed to call the Goddess, see drawing Down the Moon Positions) be respectful and humble and ask for her insights. Ask that she fill you, her child that you may do her positive works and that you may have the answers you so need. Releasing her is easy, when she is finished she will tell you and you thank her for coming and release her energy. That's it!

Wolfen Wicca 2
Class #11
Positions Drawing Down the Moon

© Lady Wolfen Mists 1992 revised 2000

Position 1 - Begin with a clearing of the mind focus on the aspect of the Goddess you wish to draw down. Head bowed and hands at your sides, feet together.

Position 2 - Raise your head to the moon and beseech the Goddess to come into you. Spread legs apart

Position 3 - Raise both hands above your hear with palms up, continue to ask the Goddess to come into you. Keep your eyes up on the moon. You may feel a tingling or such, this is the Goddess energy coming into you. Once She has been drawn down, you relax and allow her to speak or talk with you.

Class #11
Positions Drawing Down the Moon Page 2

© Lady Wolfen Mists 1992 revised 2000

Releasing The Goddess

When the Goddess is finished she will let you know, DO NOT dismiss her as you do the 4 corners in the circle. Tell her thank you for coming and she may go if she wishes, be humble and tell her that you will continue to work with in the light and do as she wishes you to.

Position 1- Thank the Goddess for coming and raise your hands once more Palms up, legs apart. Face raised to the Moon.

Position 2- Keeping your legs apart, Bring the right arm down and place palm face down on the left shoulder.

Position 3- Next bring down the left arm and place it palm down on the right shoulder . Slowly bring head down and bow you head down

Position 4- Stand for 13 heart beats with arms crossed and head down. Now bring together your legs, feel the Goddess energies leaving you. Don't worry if you cry as this is intense and emotional. You may also chant if you like or hum.

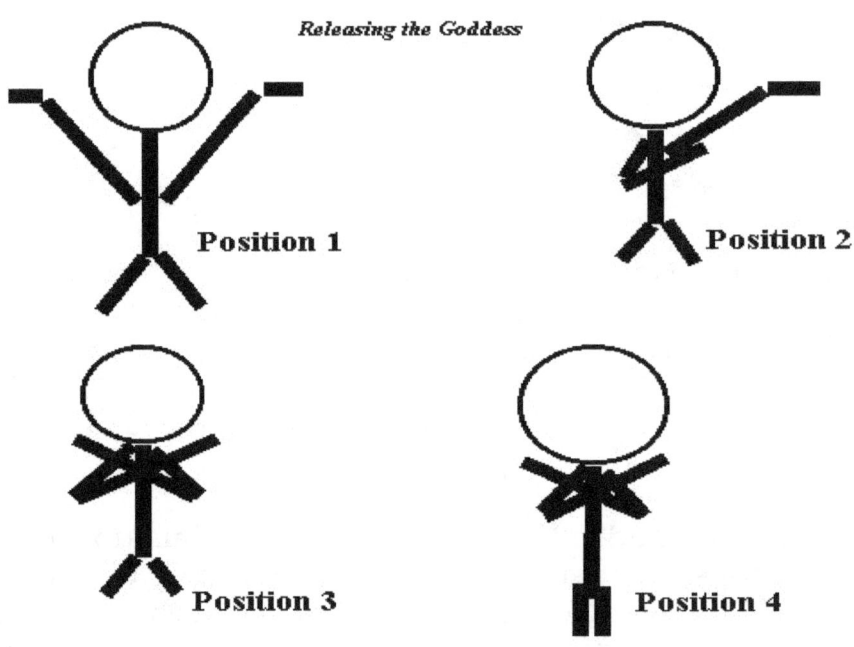

Releasing the Goddess

Position 1   Position 2   Position 3   Position 4

Wolfen Wicca 2
Class #11
Drawing Down The Moon Ritual

By Lady Wolfen Mists & Lady Shadow Stalker
c Sept. 12, 1992
revised c Dec. 2, 1996

Please note: Words in *Italic* denote an action to preform. High Priest parts start with Bold letters. High Priestess parts are Both Bold and Underlined. Any other participants are included under the title All, which is written in all capital letters.

Once the circle has been cast, all enter the circle. The altar is lit in the usual manner. *The High Priestess (facing the altar) stands* to the right side of the altar. The High priest moves to the center, front of the altar, facing the grove.

High Priest:
"As we gather tonight, We call the Goddess to join us."

(High Priest turns to face the High Priestess and continues)

"Lady of Light, on this full moon we gather as millions before us gathered, to worship and praise you. We light this special incense that it may lead you to our circle tonight."

(High Priest adds incense to charcoal)

"We practice the Mysteries of the Ages as you have   taught us. For ever in prefect Love and Trust."

High Priest takes a few steps back. The High Priestess moves toward the center of the altar. The High Priest says the following, facing the High Priestess .

Drawing Down The Moon Ritual Page 2

High Priest: *on bended knee (if possible)*
"She who is called Immortal, The Innocent "

ALL: "Hail! Goddess of Life, and Love"

High Priest:
"Giver of Life, Keeper of the Cauldron of rebirth, in its never ending cycle holding your children near."

ALL: "Hail! Mother Creatress"

High Priest:
"Mother of all Mysteries, Crone of Knowledge and Justice. Creatress of the Stars and the Moon. Called Queen of all realms."

ALL: "Hail the Triple Goddess, Come unto this sacred space.

High Priest:
"Heed the call of your children of the craft, followers of the ancient ways."

ALL: "Hail to the Bright Lady's presence!"

High Priest:
"We do invoke you, All Mother, into our High Priestess."

<u>High Priestess</u> *(with arms outstretched in Pentagram position):*
"Come Mother, Fill your earthly vessel, that I may speak your words of truth. I am Your most humble servant, Your Priestess, and I await you."

High Priest escorts High Priestess to her chair. He then kneels (or bows) before the High Priestess and says :

Class #11
Drawing Down The Moon Ritual Page 3

High Priest:
Listen to the words of the All Mother. Who men have called Diana, Isis, Demeter, Astarta, Hecate, Brigid, Cerridwen, Kali, Ananna and many others. Listen to She who IS and always will BE. Listen to the words of the All Mother."

High Priest kisses the High Priestess hand or edge of robe. Then Stands and backs away 3 paces.

High Priestess stands and invokes the pentagram over all gathered. She can continue to sit or stand as she chooses. She can begin to speak inspired words from the Mother to specific persons or as a group in general. She may or may not answer questions put to her at this time. To ask her a question one may come forward and bow or kneel, ask the question, listen and then BACK away. Do NOT turn your back on her as it is considered rude. She will decide when all has been said and then instruct the High Priest to begin the cakes and Wine Rite. The Goddess once invoked may stay the entire full moon/sabbat or she may leave when she chooses, it is up to her entirely, however if She is still there when the circle is banished be SURE that all thank her and reaffirm their devotion to her and the Old ways, this is just done as a way of expressing humility & worship..

fin.

Goddess of the Sapphire Charm

The Charge of the Goddess

Now listen to the words of the Great Mother, who was of old also called among men:
> Artemis, Astarte, Athene, Dione, Melusine, Aphrodite, Cerridwen, Dana, Arianrhod, Isis, Bride, and by many other names.
> At Her altars, the youth of Lacedaemon in Sparta made due sacrifice.

Whenever you have need of anything, once in the month, and better it be when the moon is full, then shall ye assemble in some secret place, and adore the spirit of me, who am Queen of All Witches.

There shall ye assemble, ye who are fain to learn sorcery, yet have not won its deepest secrets: to these I will teach things that are yet unknown. And ye shall be free from slavery; and as a sign that ye be really free, ye shall be naked in your rites; and ye shall dance, sing, feast, make music and love, all in my praise. For mine is the ecstasy of the spirit, and mine also is joy on Earth, for my law is love unto all beings.

Keep pure your highest ideals; strive ever towards it, let naught stop you or turn you aside; for mine is the secret door which opens unto the door of youth, and mine is the cup of wine of life, and the cauldron of Cerridwen, which is the Holy Grail of Immortality.

I am the gracious Goddess, who gives the gift of joy unto the heart of man. Upon earth, I give the knowledge of the spirit eternal; and beyond death, I give peace, and freedom, and reunion with those who have gone before.

No do I demand sacrifice; for behold, I am the Mother of all living, and my love is poured out upon the earth. Hear ye the words of the Star Goddess; she in the dust of whose feet are the hosts of heaven, whose body encircles the universe.

Pronunciation of Goddess Name

Goddess Name	Pronunciation
Artemis	Art te mus
Astarte	A Start Tay
Athene	A thea na
Dione	Dee on A
Melusine	Mil la seen
Aphrodite	Af fro di tee
Cerridwen	Care id done
Dana	Dee ann NA
Arianhod	Air rayon odd
Isis	Ice is
Bride	Br ride (or Bridge it)

 ## The Charge of The God

Listen to the words of the Great Father,
who of old was called Osiris, Adonis, Zeus, Thor, Pan, Cernunnos, Herne, Lugh
and by many other names:

My law is Harmony with all things.

Mine is the secret that opens the gates of life and mine is the dish of salt of the
earth that is the body of Cernunnos that is the eternal circle of rebirth.

I give the knowledge of life everlasting,
and beyond death I give promise of regeneration and renewal.

I am the sacrifice, the father of all things,
and my protection blankets the earth.

Hear the words of the Dancing God, the music of whose laughter stirs the wings,
hose voice calls the season:

I am the Lord of the Hunt and the Power of the Light,
sun among the clouds and the secret of the flame.

I call upon your bodies to arise and come unto me.
For I am the flesh of the earth and all its beings.
Thru me all things must die and with me are reborn.

Let my worship be in the body that sings,
for behold all acts of willing sacrifice are my rituals.

Let there be desire and fear, anger and weakness,
joy and peace, awe and longing within you.

For these too are the mysteries found within yourself,
within me,
all beginnings have endings,
and all endings have beginnings.

Wolfen Wicca 2
Class #11
Additional Sabbat Information

© Lady Wolfen Mists 1992 revised 2000

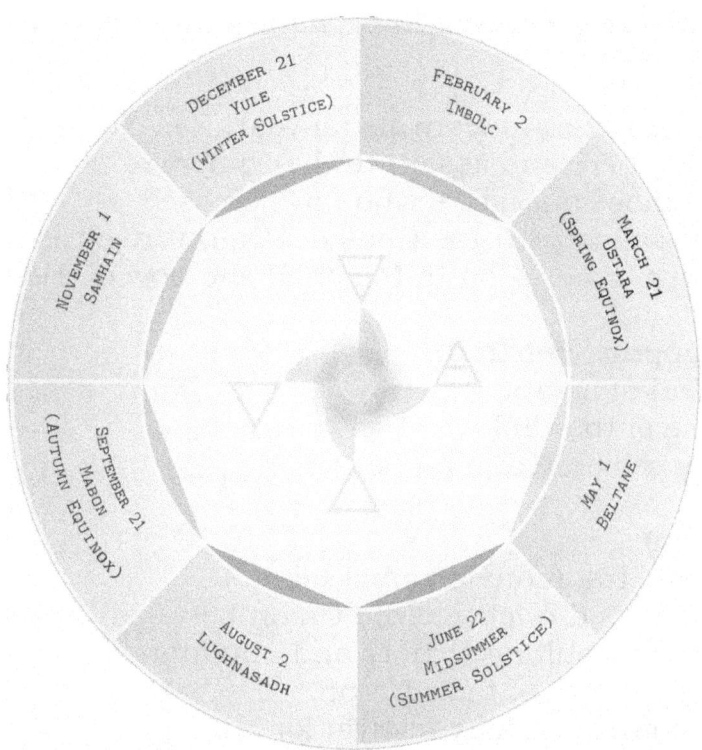

Sabbats Fall into two main categories, Greater and Lesser. In each category the male or female aspects are more dominate then the other, leading to the "Dark half" of the year and the "Light half." The following is additional information on Sabbats. The information is set up in an outline style for quick and easy reference.

Sabbats: Grand Sabbats

(1) **"Greater" also called Grand, Lunar, Seasonal Or Fire Festivals**
   (A) This is the Light Half of the year (Summer) where the Goddess and her attributes rule, but not so mush as to leave the God aspects out completely

   (B) "Calling Down the Moon" is performed at these Sabbats.

   (C) A good time for spells of Abundance and starting new things & phases in life.

Class #11
Additional Sabbat Information Page 2

(D) Fire Festivals are celebrations of Light, also when bonfires were traditionally used

(2) List of Greater Sabbats & important point pertaining to them

(A) **Samhain (Oct. 31)**
   One of the most important festivals all year: New Years.
   Death of the God here and assent to the Underworld.
   Honor given to those ancestors who have crossed.
   The Goddess is sad here at the Gods death, but rejoices in the knowledge that he will return to her soon In the child she now carries

(B) **Candlemas   (approx. Feb 2nd)**
   This is a Festival of Lights.
   Here is the time of the Child.
   The Goddess is celebrated in all her fertility.

(C) **Beltane (May 1st)**
   The May pole is a traditional symbol here.
   The Goddess and God celebrate the Union between them. and the resulting fertility and abundance to come, as a result of their Union.
   Celebrated as a grand fertility festival for all.

(D) **Lammas (Aug.1st)**
   This is the first Fire festival of the Harvest.
   Corn dollies made here from the last sheaf of corn, they are kept to ensure a fruitful & abundant harvest next year.
   Goddess is seen here in all her bounty and loving abundance.
   Feast of the Fairies (this is the best time to see them).

Sabbats: Lesser Sabbats

(1) **"Lesser" also called Solar High Days, Solar Sabbats**
   (A) This is the "Dark Half" of the year (Winter) where the God and his attributes rule, but not so much as to leave the Goddess aspects out completely.

   (B) "Calling Down the Sun" is performed at these Sabbats.

   (C) A good time to create talismans and God (male, yang) centered projects

Wolfen Wicca 2; Our Walk Onward To Initiation

Class #11
Additional Sabbat Information Page 3

  (D) Four main rites to the Sun celebrated here.

(2) List of the "Lesser Sabbats" & important points pertaining to them
  (A) **Winter Solstice Yule (approx. Dec 22nd)**
    This is the rebirth of the Sun/God who gave his life at Samhain.
    A glimmer of the return of life after a long respite.
    Shortest day of the year

  (B) **Spring Equinox Ostara (approx. March 21st)**
    Time to celebrate the resurgence and birth of life ,as the circle
     turns, to replenish earth with new life
    The day is equal to the night.

  (C) **Summer Solstice Or Midsummers (Approx. June 21st)**
    End of the Reign of the Oak King to be replaced by the Holly King (this
     varies from tradition to tradition)
    Traditionally this is the time to harvest herbs.
    Longest day of the year.

  (D) **Autumn Equinox   (Approx. Sept. 22nd)**
    The final harvest of the year
    Special reverence is given the Horned God at this time.
    There is a traditional acknowledgment of Hades taking Persephone to
     the Underworld

Lady Wolfen Mists

Wolfen Wicca 2
Class #11
Traditional Placement of Altar at Outside Sabbat

© Lady Wolfen Mists 1992 revised 2000

As the Wheel of the Year turns, the energies contained within move in a circular fashion. The same idea and energy movement can be found within the Sacred Space itself. These energies <u>ALWAYS</u> move in a deosil (clockwise) direction. To take the best advantage of the power these energies create, the altar should be placed in a specific section of the circle. Below is a diagram that shows where the altar should be located at specific Sabbat times. Remember this is for the best use of the intense energies available in this section at this time.

If it is impossible for you to move your altar from where you normally set it up, that's alright. This is just a guide to optimize the available energies, so that you can make a perfect connection to the natural energy flow. It should not however, keep you from creating your sacred space, just because you are unable to set up in a specific section. All the energy inside the circle is sphere shaped and as such the energies flow in a continues circle/ sphere shape, that is until you release the cone of power you and your actions have built.

Wolfen Wicca 2; Our Walk Onward To Initiation

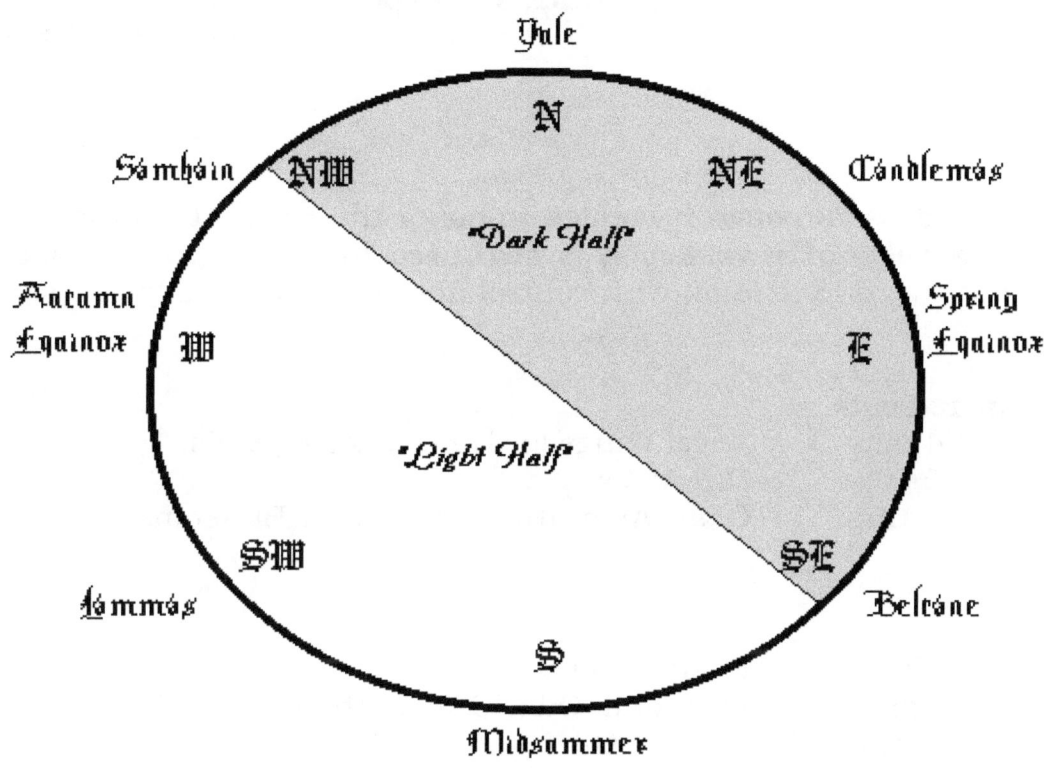

Wolfen Wicca 2
Class #11
Triple Goddess Potpourri

© Lady Wolfen Mists 1992 revised 2000

Triple Goddess Potpourri is created to honor the 3 aspects of the Bright Lady and the 3 aspects of a woman. It is also used to aid the user to successfully move about the astral realm. with control and memories easily accessible upon return

Solid Ingredients

1/4 cup	Angel Wings (or Honeysuckle petals)
1/2 cup	Oak Moss
1 Cup	Globe Amarath (or red clover Blossoms)

Oils

25 Drops	Heather Oil
2 drops	Patchouli Oil (NO more than 2 period)
10 drops	of Clove Oil
15 drops	of Ambergris Oil

Mix Oils and solid ingredients thoroughly and let "Marry" for over night. Store In a Jar (IE Mason jar) and in a cool dark place. Be sure to label with name and date created

Wolfen Wicca 2
Class # 11
The Myth of the Goddess

The following story is called "The Myth of The Goddess" and it is a slightly condensed version of a ritual story of the descent of the Goddess to the Nether Lands (Under World), as adapted by Gerald Gardner and Doreen Valiente. It is appropriate that you read it with this entire section in mind, as it exemplifies the end of spring and summer and the coming of fall and winter. The Myth of the Goddess relates story of the never ending cycle, as it closely relates to the festival of the season, Samhain.

"Now our Lady the Goddess had never loved, but She would solve all the Mysteries, even the mystery of Death; and so She journeyed to the Underworld

The Guardians of the Portals challenged Her: "Strip off thy garments, lay aside thy jewels; for naught mayest thou bring with thee into this our land."

So She laid down her garments and Her jewels, and was bound, as are all who enter the Realms of Death, the Mighty One.

Such was Her beauty, that Death Himself knelt and kissed Her feet, saying: "Blessed be thy feet, that have brought thee in these ways. Abide with me; but let me place my cold hand on thy heart."

Myth of the Goddess Page 2

She replied: "I love thee not. Why dost thou cause all things that I love and take delight in to fade and die?"

"Lady," replied Death, "'tis age and fate, against which I am helpless. Age causes all to wither; but when men die at the end of time, I give them rest and peace, and strength so that they may return. But thou! Thou art lovely. Return not; abide with me!" But She answered: "I love thee not."

Then said Death: "An thou receivest not my hand on thy heart, thou must receive Death's scourge."

"It is fate better so," She said. And She knelt, and Death scourged her tenderly. And She cried, "I feel the pangs of love."

And Death said, "Blessed be!" and gave her the Fivefold Kiss, saying: "Thus only mayest thou attain to joy and knowledge." And He taught Her all the Mysteries, and They so loved and were one, and He taught Her all the Magics.

For there are three great events in the life of man: Love, Death, and Resurrection in the new body; and Magic controls them all. For to fulfill love you must return again at the same time and place as the loved one, and you must remember and love them again. But to be reborn you must die and be ready for a new body; and to die you must be born; and without love you may not be born; and this is all the Magics. "

Wolfen Wicca 2
Class #11
Practical; Drawn Down The Moon

© Lady Wolfen Mists Jan.1992
revised 2015

Instructions to the Practical Section

Do a circle cast and mock walk through of Drawing Down the Moon How did it go? What energies did you feel? Did you make a connection the the Bright Lady in any way?

Notes for My First Drawing Down The Moon

Notes For Class 11

Lady Wolfen Mists

Wolfen Wicca 2
Our Walk Onward To Initiation
Class #12

© Lady Wolfen Mists Jan.1990

Theory:
Long Rede
Its all in the Perspective
DARKNESS vs Dark/shadow self; What they are
5 Fold Kiss
Traditions
Coven Offices

Practical:
Amulet for Good Luck

Circle Work:
What is your inspirational thought for the week.

***Assignment: **Students in your Magickal Journal:**
Make an Amulet for Good Luck. How did it go? What did you feel when creating it. This will be reviewed when you submit your work for Initiation ☺

"I Walk On!

Wolfen Wicca 2
Class #12
26 stanza Long Wiccan Rede

This is the 26 stanza version of the Wiccan Rede which was authored by Adriana Porter, maternal Grand mother of Gwen Thompsen, one of the three non-Gardnerian Priestess who founded NECTW (The New England Coven of Traditionalist Witches) of New England. Gwen Published the Rede by itself in Green Egg in the early 1970's

The Wiccan Rede

Bide the Wiccan laws ye must,
in perfect love and perfect trust.

Live and let live -
fairly take and fairly give.

Cast the Circle thrice about
to keep all evil spirits out.

To bind the spell every time,
let the spell be spake in rhyme.

Soft of eye and light of touch -
speak ye little, listen much.

Lady Wolfen Mists

<u>26 stanza Long Wiccan Rede Page 2</u>

*Deosil go by the waxing Moon -
sing and dance the Wiccan Rune.*

*Widdershins go when the Moon doth wane,
and the werewolf howls by the dread wolfsbane.*

*When the Lady's Moon is new,
kiss the hand to Her times two.*

*When the Moon rides at Her peak,
then your heart's desire seek.*

*Heed the North wind's mighty gale -
lock the door and drop the sail.*

*When the wind comes from the South,
love will kiss thee on the mouth.*

*When the wind blows from the East,
expect the new and set the feast.*

*When the West wind blows o'er thee,
departed spirits restless be.*

*Nine woods in the Cauldron go -
burn them quick and burn them slow.*

*Elder be ye Lady's tree -
burn it not or cursed ye'll be.*

*When the Wheel begins to turn,
let the Beltane fires burn.*

*When the Wheel has turned a Yule,
lighty the Log and let Pan rule.*

*Heed ye flower, bush and tree -
by the Lady blessed be.*

Wolfen Wicca 2; Our Walk Onward To Initiation

26 stanza Long Wiccan Rede Page 3

Where the rippling waters go,
cast a stone and truth ye'll know.

When ye are in dire need,
hearken not to others' greed.

With the fool no season spend,
or be counted as his friend.

Merry meet and merry part -
bright the cheeks and warm the heart.

When misfortune is enow,
wear the blue star on thy brow.

True in love ever be,
unless thy lover's false to thee.

Eight words the Wiccan Rede fulfill -
<u>*an ye harm none, do what ye will*</u>*.*

Wolfen Wicca 2
Class #12
All In the Perspective- A Christians Question

©by Lady Wolfen Mists   June 6 2004 2:34 am

Someone from a main stream Christian religion once asked me if I believed in Miracles and Angels and do I pray when I speak to God? He said he had come to this witch shop to talk to the top witch and that he firmly believed that witches should die because the bible said so, "Suffer ye not a witch to live!"

At that moment I wondered at the wisdom of the Lady and Lord to use me as their vessel in this case. Would I be smart enough or patient enough to answer as my Lady would wish me, would I represent the Wolfen Wicca tradition and the pagan community as they would wish? I took a deep breath and said to the Lady silently. "If you want me to do this I will need your help with speech and guidance."

Then I took another breath and asked him into my office so we could be comfortable while we talked. He wanted the door left open, I guess he thought my "evil" wouldn't dare touch him with the door open and while he clutched his bible. I not only left the door open I placed his chair in front of it so he would feel more secure about being there and asking his questions. Next I answered his questions calmly and completely.

"Yes I do believe in miracles, those times in life when things are prefect or work out for the highest blessing for all involved. Miracles when so many energies combine as one, with the universe energies, to produce the best most wanted outcome of it all even in a situation even when said situation was the most distressing, no way out times in our lives. Miracles, those times in life when for a few

Wolfen Wicca 2; Our Walk Onward To Initiation

All In the Perspective- A Christians Question Page 2

seconds, we reach an understanding of the vast abilities of the Creators. When the plan of the universe seems, for a fleeting second to make sense, when we see the true beauty that abounds about us, and have a deep understanding of it all. Miracles when unconditional love no longer seems a word out there to strive for, but is a real tangible living thing that we can feel and wrap ourselves and others in. Yes I do most deeply and ardently believe in miracles.

Angels- without a doubt I believe in Angels, those masters that went before me who guide me and help me make the best journey I can. Spirit Guides who bless me and keep me from harm, entities who are so positive in nature that they make me, in mortal form weep, and wish I to could be as they. Angles who on earth help me (and others) in the most unexpected times and ways. Angels who work the will of the loving Lady and Lord and guide me down the Higher Self path so that I may ascend on my spiritual journey. Yes I do without a doubt believe in angels and I often speak and confer with them on many many things.

Pray- Yes I do pray. Every time I cast a spell it is a prayer for the aid of the Lady and Lord. Do I pray in humility to the Goddess and God? I do, and even more so when on the astral or within my circle, when I come into their presence and spend time with them. If it be as they feed me cookies and milk healing my hurts or as they teach me their ways down the lighted path or even as they give me my next lesson or job to learn. Yes I do it with love and humility. Do I pray for help when in need to them, yes when in fear I call to my Lord or my Lady I beg for them to lift me up and protect me I ask that they fill me with their white light and keep me from harm. I pray in my daily devotions for this same loving help and direction for all my friends and family. I also pray for the world in general and for those who do not understand, so that their hearts may be open to the Lighted path of my most loving Lady and Lord.

This answer so astounded this Christian, he didn't know what else to say. Soon he stumbled, stuttered and muttered to himself. Then he said "But your a Witch, your evil!" I laughed and said "Then so must you be cause we both believe in miracles, angels and we both pray to the Creators of life and the universe. We both seek for the Lighted ways and we both wish only the best for those we love, that no harm or hurt or negativity ever befall them or us (if we can help it).

You see it is all perspective that leads the heart. We all walk paths, much the same but different for each individual. Just because the Creators saw to making your path different from mine didn't mean that all such other paths or peoplc are evil. No not at all, it just means that as the Lady and Lord who created all things with great uniqueness and difference, so did they create ways for each of us to reach them, love them and share in the Blessings and Unconditional love they give us all." This seemed to astound him even more and for the next several months he came to my office at the store asking real questions and sharing insights. Education does

All In the Perspective- A Christians Question Page 3

wonders to tearing down walls and fears.

I did not change him from Christian to Wiccan (I did not wish to for Christian was where the Universe best placed him) but I did open his eyes and his heart. At the end of it all he told me he would no longer follow the belief "Suffer ye not a witch to live!" That he liked and respected me and didn't see any evil in our religion, just another way to God. I cried for his eyes were opened, we could continue to share and the Lady and Lord had used me (this mortal vessel) to work Their will once more! I was glad I had done as They had asked even when I wasn't sure I was up to the task. I was even happier that we had shared questions, answers and made a friendship.

So next time someone questions you, even though you may wonder how in the world could they believe that about you or you wonder if you should waste the time answering. Take a moment and see if this is a time you to can change a perspective, open eyes and teach another about the wonders of being different but alike. Take a second before you lash out at that <u>stupid question</u> and **THINK**, this could be a turning point for this person, you may be being called upon to be an angel on earth to teach and share and build bridges and not make walls. Maybe you too are a vessel the Lady and Lord will use. try compassion before anger and openness when you can. Who knows this may very well be a lesson for you also.

Many Blessings to all
LWM

Wolfen Wicca 2
Class #12
DARKNESS vs Dark/shadow self; What they are

by Lady Wolfen Mists 11/25/2014

OK no more putting it off, here is what the Angels have been pushing me to write. The Difference between the DARKNESS and the dark/shadow self. I haven't wanted to write it cause I know its gonna open a can of worms and I am not really up to the arguments, but one can not fight the Angels, they always win with me. So angels let your energies flow and lets get started.

Lets start with the shadow self and what that is by my definition. It is the dark half of the self we all have, the Negative polarity wise, that we are all born with. It is a part of you and must be honored, just as the Light half or Positive half is honored. One should never strive to remove the dark half of the self for that would put the soul out of sync and not be true to who you are. Sure the dark half is there and we all sometimes have dark, sad hurtful thoughts. But we Choose not to dwell in them and to keep ourselves balanced. Without the dark half we would not feel pain at the crossing of a loved one, or cry when we hurt. There is a balance that is struck within us between the positive and negative polarities and we work to keep that balance. I have never promoted that one should totally remove the dark/shadow self but one should work within the light and keep all things balanced. The dark/shadow self has its place and is kept there, it does not war with the light and lives side by side when both are in tune. If either side positive or negative is related to too much and allowed to control the self then that also is bad for the self. All things in moderation and that includes both the polarities we are all born with. Acknowledge within the dark/shadow self and let your actions be those that helps keep you on the lighted path. Just because you acknowledge the dark part of the self and honor it does not mean you have to choose to live there in the dark half.

Now on to the DARKNESS. The DARKNESS is an entity/energy in the universe that is not content to lay side by side with the LIGHT. It wants to control and feed off the LIGHT, wants to destroy all LIGHT and has no room for anything else. The DARKNESS is not willing to compromise, it's one ultimate task is to bring hurt and pain to all. The DARKNESS finds joy, happiness and bliss in keeping so many from their spiritual path and away from a spiritual connection to the Creator(s). The DARKNESS is always in battle with the LIGHT and will attack anyone or anything that works for the LIGHT. The DARKNESS feeds off of us, off our fear, anger, hurt, depression, drug use and anything else that might tie us down to the lower levels of being. One can not reason with the DARKNESS for it is centered on harming all and feeding off of them, controlling their every action. Once done it moves on to the next. All that can be done is to Battle the DARKNESS and send it back to the Universe so that its energy can be reused in a more positive manner that would help everyone.

DARKNESS vs Dark/shadow self; Page 2

Have you never noticed that often when you do something good for another that something bad comes seeking you? That is the DARKNESS keeping you from doing more Lighted positive things, Do these things anyway for it lifts your very soul and those you help. The DARKNESS can not have this so it puts obstacles and painful things in your way to get you to refocus your energy. To keep you from helping others and to think only of your problems. When this happens STOP! Take a deep breath and say "DARKNESS I know you are there. I will not serve you, I will not fear you. I will fight again and again no matter how many times I fall, for I am a servant of the Light and Positive path" The battle to keep the DARKNESS from taking your soul (feeding off of it and confining you to these lower realms of being) is on going and if you are a Light Warrior or a Light Worker you know what I am trying to say. We must not let this Darkness win or we (all beings who live in this realm) are doomed to remain separated from the Higher more spiritual realms and serving the DARKNESS as it feeds off our very life essence.

Ok you say, I get that, but what can I a single person do? Do good things, reach out when you can, show compassion, sing, be joyful, be grateful, lift others up, find your spiritual center and work from there, practice acceptance of others, and above all LOVE. That my friends will not just remove the DARKNESS (and send it to be reused in a more positive way by the universe) It will also lift this whole plane of existence up to higher levels, bringing us closer to the Creator(s) and to our true Higher Self's.

Well now that is done and it wasn't as hard as I thought it would be. There is much more in depth but for many of you I hope this will be enough to get the point across. No one is asking you to deny your shadow/dark self or not to be all of who you are. No! We are asking you to join in with this battle against the DARKNESS and help lift this world/plane to a higher level. To be balanced in your actions/work and LOVE, that is all.

Wolfen Wicca 2
Class 12
5 Fold Kiss

(c) Lady Wolfen Mists 2005

In many of your reading and in exploring other traditions of Wicca you may run across references to The 5 Fold Kiss. It is usually preformed by Gardnerian and Alexandrian covens but other traditions do use it. It most often used in the Drawing Down The Moon rites as well as handfasting's and such rite. Sometimes you may see it referred to as the 5 Fold Salute, Wiccan Salute as well as the 5 Fold Kiss. Although this is usually preformed skyclad , it is NOT sexual in nature and is used with respect and great esteem. Great homage paid by the Goddess and God to each other. in this rite The five fold kiss may only be conducted man to woman or woman to man. The kisses correspond to the pentacle. Each kiss is accompanied by a blessing.

The Kiss its self is comprised of 5 positions on the body in which the High Priest administers the kiss while invoking the powers that be. It starts on the right side each time and then goes to the left, although there are actually 5 positions as mentioned there are a total of 8 kisses delivered. The High Priest kisses the High Priestess on both feet, both knees, womb, both breasts, and ends with the lips.

****

5 Fold for High Priestess

The rite goes like this. Please Note there are variations for different traditions but you will get the idea:

5 Fold Kiss Page 2

The High Priestess stands with her legs and arms outstretched. The High Priest kneels before the High Priestess and kisses her right foot, then her left. He says;
"Blessed be thy feet, that have brought thee in these ways.

He then Kisses her right knee then her left and says;
"Blessed be thy knees, that shall kneel at the sacred altar."

Moving on he kisses her frontal womb area and states;
"Blessed be thy womb, without which we would not be."

Next he kisses her right breast and the left breast and states
"Blessed be thy breasts, formed in beauty."

Finally he kisses her lips and says;
"Blessed be thy lips, that shall utter the Sacred Names."

When this is completed the High Priest Kneels once more in front but off to the side of the High Priestess, who now takes the Drawing Down the Moon Positions, with her right foot slightly forward.. The High Priest begins the words for Drawing down the moon.

That is all their is to the 5 fold kiss. Now before you ask their is also a 5 Fold Kiss for the High Priest often used in Drawing Down the Sun. It is pretty much the same except the womb becomes the phallus.

****

5 Fold for High Priest

The High Priestess kneels before the High Priest who has both legs and arms outstretched;

She Kisses his right foot then left and says:
"Blessed be thy feet, that have brought thee in these ways."

Next She kisses both Knees, right then left and states;
"Blessed be thy knees, that shall kneel at the sacred altar."

She then kisses the outside of the phallus and says;
"Blessed be thy phallus, without which we would not be."

5 Fold Kiss Page 3

She moves on the the right then left breast and states;
"Blessed be thy breasts, formed in strength."

Finally she kisses His Lips saying;
"Blessed be thy lips, that shall utter the Sacred Names."

When this is completed the High Priestess kneels once more in front but off to the side of the High Priest, who now takes the Drawing Down the Sun Positions. The High Priestess begins the words for Drawing down the Sun.

****

So after reading the rite one could see how it could easily be misinterpreted by outsiders and maligned. Also many people do NOT wish to be sky clad so this rite can be done with a wand pointing at the places that are to be kissed, keeping the boundaries of everyone intact. We at Wolfen Wicca just do not preform the 5 fold kiss as many of the acting High Priests and High Priestess are students in training and uncomfortable with this rite. If the High Priestess and High Priest are uncomfortable with the rite then that places obstacles in the Drawing Down section and it will not be successful. So we just don't use this rite. However as well rounded students I felt you had reason to be informed of it and how it works. It is a part of Wiccan History. Just as a side fact some people believe that the term "**Blessed Be**" originated from the 5 Fold Kiss and was used in respect to the Goddess and God.

Wolfen Wicca 2
Class #12
Traditions

Have you ever had anyone come up to you and say: "What tradition do follow?" Not wanting to look like an idiot you mumble something about, "the old ways" and walk away scratching your head. Exactly what is a tradition anyway? Is it something that all Wiccans have and just don't know it? Is it sorta like that thing where all Wiccans are pagans but not all pagans are Wiccans??? Well its really pretty simple, a tradition is like a denomination that you follow. Its a system under Wicca that someone has been know to follow, or in some cases not follow, specific guidelines/rules. Traditions vary as much as covens do, meaning looking at 100 of either one and you will find 100 different ways of doing something. But traditions usually stay fairly close to certain guidelines set down by its founder.

The following is a brief overview of a **few** of the more popular traditions. Like I said there are many more, but this will get you started and next time someone asks you can give an intelligent answer!

Alexandrian Wicca

Founded by Alex Sanders (England). Alex claimed the title of "King" of the Witches. Rituals are basically modified from Gardnerian tradition. Practitioners of this style usually practice skyclad. They celebrate 8 Sabbaths, and the Goddess & God are equally honored.

Wolfen Wicca 2; Our Walk Onward To Initiation

Traditions Page 2

American Celtic Wicca

Founded by Lady Sheba (Jessica Ball). Lady Sheba claimed the title of "Queen of the Witches". Rituals are based on Gardner's. Robes are the traditional garb here. There are 8 sabbats that are celebrated with the God & Goddess being equally honored.

British Traditional

This is combination of Celtic and Gardnerian styles. Some of the more famous followers of this style are the authors Janet and Stewart Farrar. Excellent writers, read their stuff if you get a chance. There are 8 Sabbaths here and Goddess & God are equal.

Celtic Wicca

This system of magick reflects an ancient pantheon of Celtic/Druid God/dess. This tradition is very much based in the power of nature, the calling of the elements and the "unseen" beings that share our world. It stress the interconnectedness of all things human and non and the importance of respect and working together. Ritual styles vary from traditional Gardnerian to open eclectic. The sabbats celebrated are usually 8 and the God Goddess are equally honored.

Ceremonial Witchcraft

This is a very ridged system of magick with lots of structure and details. The Kabbalah can be found under this tradition as well as some forms of Greek & Egyptian systems. Sabbats celebrated here vary with tradition. The focus of the Goddess & God also varies.

Dianic Wicca (also sometimes called Feminist Wicca)

This tradition was pointed out by Margaret Murry (1921) currently the tradition claims to have been founded by Ann Forfreedom. There is alot of focus on female aspects and leadership here. But in most covens who follow Dianic Wicca the male energies are not totally disregarded. Covens vary in that they can be female only or co-ed, but they are not necessarily lesbian in nature. The rituals are typically eclectic, coven members may be robed or sky clad. They commonly celebrate 8 Sabbats, with an emphasis on the Goddess.

Eclectic Wicca

This system of magick is a combination of many systems. Basically the practitioner uses "what works best" for them. No particular tradition or pantheon observed here. Sabbats celebrated are usually 8 in number. The Goddess and God are equally honored in this tradition.

Traditions Page 3

Gardnerian Wicca

Founded by Gerald Gardner (1950) who brought this tradition out of the shadows and into the public light. in the 1950's in England. It is my opinion that Gerald Gardner was instrumental in keeping Wicca, as we know it today, alive and working. The rituals are very structured in nature, and the members are sworn to secrecy. Practitioners are usually skyclad, they have a formal degree system. This degree system doesn't allow for any type of self-initation by practitioners. they celebrate 8 sabbats. They also focus more on the Goddess energies but not so much as to exclude the God energies.

Georgian Wicca

Founded by George Patterson. This tradition is very eclectic, often drawing from the Alexandrian and Gardnerian styles. However it is not in any way limited to these types of structured magickal systems. Practitioners are usually, but not necessarily, skyclad. This tradition was first charted as a church, the Church of Wicca of Bakersfield, Ca, in 1972. Then it was revised as the Georgian Church in 1980. They celebrate 8 main Sabbats. The Goddess is focused on more then the God.

Northern Way

This system of Magick follows the Norse system (Asatru), and was founded around 1980. It is a non-degreed non-initiatory tradition. Practitioners usually wear ancient Norse clothing & robes. Typically when casting a circle they do not call the 4 quarters at all. There are 4 Solar Fire festivals observed as well as a few other Norse celebrations. In this Tradition the God is focused upon more than the goddess, but no so much as to exclude the Goddess completely.

Seax- Wica

Founded by Raymond Buckland in 1973. Based upon the Saxon tradition, but was developed as a whole denomination in and of itself. Buckland used only the traditional Saxon deity names, in creating this totally new magickal system. Practitioners can work robed or sky-clad. It tradition is considered a democratic organization, (no coven leaders), all rituals are published and available to anyone, room for both Coven Initiation and Self Initiation. There are 8 main Sabbats and the God and Goddess are equally honored.

Strega Witches

This is a system of magick from Italy, around 1353-1354. Aradia plays a very important and central part in this tradition. Practitioners can practice sky clad or robed. I recommend checking this system out, if for nothing more then reading the beautifully written rite & rituals. There are 8 main Sabbats. The focus here is on the Goddess, but the God is honored also.

Wolfen Wicca 2; Our Walk Onward To Initiation

Traditions Page 4

Wolfen Wicca

This Sect of Wicca was founded by Lady Wolfen Mists in the late 1980's early 1990's, as a total new inspired style of Wicca. It is formal system that is trademarked. In essence the entire system is very secretive in nature, and the members are sworn to secrecy. There is a ranking system of degrees, that doesn't allow for any type of advancement through or using just self-initiation by practitioners. **All students must rise through the degrees** of the system set up for everyone. Practitioners are usually in formal robes when conducting rituals or rites. Mostly eclectic in nature, Wolfen Wicca does celebrate the 13 full moons, 8 Sabbats a year with an emphasis on both the God and Goddess, leading to the equal importance of both male and female roles in Wicca.

Wolfen Wicca 2
Class #12

Pagans who made the road easier for us all

Gerald Gardener   An English hereditary Witch, founder of contemporary Witchcraft practiced as a religion (Gardenerian Tradition). Some think he was a wonderful visionary, others think he was a dark power monger who manipulated many a student. No matter what one can not get away from his importance in the re emergence of Wicca His tradition is usually performed Sky Clad

Dione Fortune – Student of Gardner. Developed her own tradition and was unconcerned with the need for publicity. Dion was a respected psychiatrist, occultist and author who approached magick and hermetic concepts from the perspectives of Jung and Freud.

Alex Sanders (AKA "King of the Witches") He became known - was responsible for founding the Alexandrian Tradition of Wicca, now one of the main traditions of the Wicca/Witchcraft movement. But his reign was fraught with criticism and controversy.

Aleister Crowley- The Great Beast" and "The Wickedest Man in the   World", Crowley was a powerful magician, poet, prophet and famed occultist. He was also a one-time witch, though most of the elders of the craft would discredit him the title.

Gavin & Yvonne Frost   Early 1970's. Gavin and Yvonne Frost are openly professed Witches, Co-founders of the first legally   recognized School and Church of Wicca in America

Doreen Valiente   Gerald Gardner's best known High   Priestess and godmother of wicca

Raymond Buckland   Wiccan author. Introduced Gardnerian wicca to   the USA. Founder of Seax Wicca

Scott Cunningham best Author ever (in my opinion)! Scott was a   key player in opening up Wicca to solitary practice, and by making a great deal of   information available to the public he helped to influence many newcomers   entering the craft.

Stewart & Janet Farrar   English author of books on Alexandrian Wicca. Stewart and wife, Janet Farrar. Since their initiation into witchcraft by Alex Sanders in February 1970, and starting their own coven in December the same year have been very significant elders/leaders in the pagan community. Stewart passed to the

Wolfen Wicca 2; Our Walk Onward To Initiation

Pagans Who made the road easier Page 2

Summerland in feb 7 2000 Janet married Gavin Bone on may 5 2001. Now Janet and Gavin continue to work on teaching and sharing.

Laurie Cabot American Witch, author, artist and businesswoman. She is the founder of the 'Cabot Science Tradition of Witchcraft' and the 'Witches League for Public Awareness (WLPA)'. As a prominent civil rights activist she founded the WLPA as a watchdog to act as an anti-defamation organization aimed at correcting many misconceptions about Witchcraft.

Otter (Oberon) Zell-Ravenheart (also known as: Tim Zell, Otter G'Zell and Oberon Zell), is a Founding member of the Church of All Worlds and a leading figure in the American Neo-Pagan community. His wife is also a famouse artist and mover in the pagan community called Morning Glory zell

Isaac Bonewits One of the more influential and colourful figures in the present day American Pagan movement. Pagan, Priest, Author, Scholar, Bard, Activist and leader in contemporary Paganism, Bonewits has dedicated his life to reviving Druidry as a religion protecting Mother Nature and all her children.

Starhawk- Author of Goddess studies and earth based studies Starhawk co-founded and co-teaches Earth Activist Training. So much more than a typical permaculture design certification course,

OK that's enough, there are tons more that I have left out but this will give you a reference to work from and explore the rest for yourself. If you want more names google Famous Wiccan people or witches, pagan people. That should give you a start

Wolfen Wicca 2
Class #12
Different types of Offices in Various Covens

The following list gives the titles and a brief description of offices held by members of a coven/grove. These are fairly traditional in nature and can be adjusted to fix you and your members as you see fit.

Offices in a traditional all women's Grove/Coven

Maiden- alternate to Mother figure, calls the members when all is ready. Does the administrative duties like letting members know who, what when where and why. Responsible for collection of dues and any special needs to be preformed at circle

Mother- Acts as the High Priestess, Oversees that all rituals and activities are "on track".

Crone- Does most of the teaching and guidance as needed. Usually a Mother/ High Priestess that has stepped down, acts as council to the Mother. Much respect is given her and her ideas at this stage.

Officers in a traditional mixed Coven/Grove

High Priestess- This is the main office of responsibility, She acts as the focus of energies of the Goddess herself on the physical plane. She is considered the minister of this religion, her duties include, Counseling, guidance, teaching, rituals like handfastings, and much more. All these responsibilities are preformed with respect to the High Priest's opinions. But remember Her word is Law! Emblem of her office includes a crescent Moon circlet(crown), Jet and Amber necklace, Ring of position(usually crescent or pentagram)

High Priest- This office is usually preformed under the direction and in agreement with what the High Priestess wishes. His duties can also include many of the items listed above but, his energies are those of the God on the physical

Wolfen Wicca 2; Our Walk Onward To Initiation

Different types of Offices in Various Covens Page 2

plane. Emblem of his office includes any horned Circlet or Helmet, or animal mask or animal cape.

Maiden- She is usually someone who is studying to become a high Priestess and acts as an alternate when the High Priestess cant be there or wants her to. She is also in charge of making sure all the domestic duties are done, like clean up after festivals. She doesn't necessarily do this but has made arraignments to see that it is done. Emblem of her office is usually a Silver Circlet or Star Tiara, also a Cauldron necklace or Broom necklace

Summoner- He is usually someone who is studying to become a High Priest and acts as an alternate when the High Priest cant be there or wants him to. His regular duties include summoning members to the circle, getting out information on anything to do with circle, collection of dues, passing out song books, rites, and information needed. He acts as contact person for information about the up coming events for coven/grove members. Emblem of office can be a silver bell or a blackthorn, or ironwood staff.

Fetch- This is usually a male member who is initiated and who works as a liaison between the coven/grove and the High Priestess. At festivals he gets Her food, drink and sees to her needs. Acts almost as a champion for High Priestess He is Her eyes and ears and keeps Her informed of all the good things and bad things he hears. He is trusted completely and does as She needs. Once a fetch has been named to the High Priestess he usually remains so even when High Priestess moves to Crone stage.

Then there is the Council of Elders found in both mixed and single sex covens/groves. I have just named them and their positions as they are fairly self explanatory.

Bardic Archivist---Group Historian

Bard Story Teller---Shares in oral and written tradition the stories of the group and the Goddess and God

Bardic Musician- Collects writes and sings songs and music for the group.

Grove Tender or Watchman---Sets up altar, checks doors, locks and curtains Acts as a sergeant at arms. In training for High Priest

Lady Wolfen Mists

Different types of Offices in Various Covens Page 3

Some of the more popular fields of study in Traditional Covens/Groves. There can be many others but these are some that you will find in most traditions.

Divinatory arts
Herbalism
Healing Animal or Familiar Arts
Ritual & Rite construction
Ritual Tools construction
Mediumship
Music
Psychic Incantation/Evocation arts
Spell Work

Wolfen Wicca 2
Class # 12
Practical: Amulet For Good Luck

© Lady Wolfen Mists 1989

Below is the general overall outline used for the practical section of this class. I've included this so if you have a specific question you can go directly to that section and find the answer quickly. I hope you find it helpful.

1. Purpose:
2. Items Included:
3. Special Information:
4. Steps to Preparation:
5. Special Storage Needs:
6. Clean Up:
7. Recharge Procedure

1) This amulet is meant to be carried in your purse or backpack. It is meant to attract good luck to is carrier. As it is an amulet, it can be used by many people, since it was not specifically created for one individual in particular.

2) Items Needed
   1 small bottle with lid
   Enough Rainwater to fill bottle
   2-4 Garnet or Opal or Amethyst Chips
   (chips must be small enough to fit in bottle)

3) This amulet be started the day before the full moon, and finished up on the full moon.

Lady Wolfen Mists

Practical: Amulet For Good Luck Page 2

4) **Steps:**
    A. The first step is to collect enough rainwater and fill your small jar/bottle. You can also use melted snow if you cant find rainwater.
Since it is very difficult to plan to plan when it may rain or may not rain, you may collect your rainwater many days in advance. Just store it in a jar in the fridge to keep it fresh.

    B. While filling the bottle with rainwater say the following:
> "*Good luck to my side fly,*
> Like the rain that falls from the sky.
> Bring only good and positive,
> So good fortune with me shall live."

    C. Pick up the stone chips and add them to the bottle. As you are placing them in the bottle, say the following;
> " *Stones of luck they may be,*
> Good luck will surly come to me.
> Amulet that I have created,
> Make all true that I have stated.
> Empowered by my energies,
> I bid you now to come to me.
> Conjured for all to see,
> As I have done it , So Mote It Be!"

That's all there is to it, your amulet is complete. Use it with wisdom and may happiness be yours..

5) Nothing special

6) Clean up as usual

7) To re-power this item all you need to do is to sit it in the moonlight, any phase, overnight.

Notes On Class 12

Lady Wolfen Mists

Wolfen Wicca 2
Our Walk Onward To Initiation
Class #13

Theory

    Degree Symbols
    Poppet Use
    Poppet Pattern
    Poppet Protection
    Poppet get Money
    Asking Directions
    What is a Triskele (Trisklion)
    Facial Analysis

Practical:
    Create a Poppet

Circle Work:
    What is your inspirational thought for the week.

***Assignment: **Students in your Magickal Journal:**
    Create a poppet of your choice here or one of your own creation, How did it go? Do you like the use of poppets? This will be reviewed when you submit your work for Initiation ☺

"I Walk On!"

Wolfen Wicca 2
Class #13
Degree Symbols

© Lady Wolfen Mists Jan.1990
revised 2001

These are symbols that are often used to denote degree and rank:

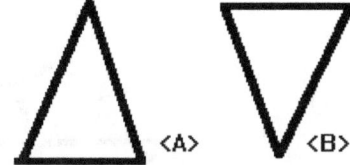

First Degree or New Initiate denotes any 1st

2nd Degree symbols
A&B-Usually denote High Priest   C-Usually denotes High Priestess
All can be worn by any 2nd degree if they wish to wear them

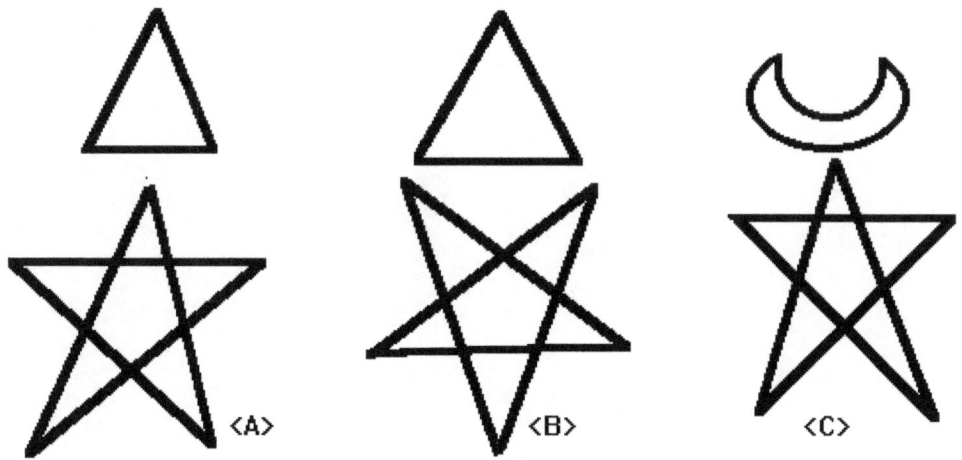

Symbols for 3rd Degree or Elder A&B all 3rds can wear C-High Priestess
3rd degree only

Lady Wolfen Mists

Class #13
Degree Symbols page 2

Sometimes 3rd Degree Crone　　　　　　　　Sometimes 3rd Degree Sage
Some Traditions use for 4 th degree　A-High Priestess　　B-High Priest

Wolfen Wicca 2
Class #13
Use of Poppets

By Lady Wolfen Mists © 1990

There is much superstition and folk lore connected with Poppets also called Voodoo Dolls, unfortunately most of it is negative in nature. Most people think Poppet Dolls are only used to exact revenge, hex, or cause harm. While it is true that they can be used for this, it is also true that they can be used for many more positive reasons. Remember that the doll is only a symbol for your magickal intent to focus on, that the real results will truly effect another individual. I would also like to deeply caution anyone who would consider using a doll in any negative way (including but not limited to: revenge, hexes, hurting another, taking another's choices like in a binding or such) to think it over **VERY CAREFULLY** before you put your thoughts into actions. Remember the 3 fold law, what ever you do positive or negative, will be returned to you in this life 3 fold and maybe even 10 fold in another life. That all your actions, both the positive & negative, in life build Karma (Universal consequences for your actions and decisions) and that Karma will have to be dealt with at sometime in your existence. You choose the karma you build, so build a strong positive foundation for your spiritual essence to grow from!

Now there are many types of Poppet/Voodoo Dolls to choose from. Just to name of few of the more popular types: there are wax dolls, paper, cloth, straw, or wood, and so on. No one type is really any better than any other type; it all really depends on the ones you feel most comfortable with. I like to use cloth dolls, as I can include what the colors of the cloth mean, as I visualize & saturate the doll with qualities, and characteristics I need to complete my spell with success. Dolls work well in any form, but unlike many other forms of magick, which ask for secrecy for success. Dolls work even better if the "target" person knows that the doll is being used as a symbol of them.

Class #13
Use of Poppets page 2

STEP #1 PERSONALIZING YOUR DOLL
The doll you create should have a specific color for a specific reason and is considered "energy clean" meaning that it is ready to use without worrying about the need for cleansing or consecrating at his point. To insure success of your doll you do need to do a few things to personalize the doll to your spell. I suggest that if at all possible you collect hair or nail clippings, or pieces of clothing or anything that the "target" person may have come into contact with. Then slit a small seam into the back of the doll and place the items you have collected there. Sew up the seam with the same color thread (or as close as you can get, when in doubt use white thread) as the doll. If you are unable to collect anything that the "target" person has touched, and this can include a sample of their handwriting or e mails, then you can paste their face on the front of the dolls face. For example you can cut out the "target" persons face from a picture, and that will serve as a symbol of who the person will be. Once you have done this you can continue with the specific spell you have intended the doll for.

STEP #2 GENERAL DIRECTIONS
When working with a doll in general you need to spend time in the Visualization of the target person's qualities and characteristics being "set" within the doll. To do this after you have completed the step of personalizing the doll, you should place the doll in both hands and close your eyes, "see" the person the spell is targeted for, and see all their qualities and characteristics, see yourself placing those same qualities and characteristics into the doll you are holding. See the doll becoming "them" in your minds eye, see a long blue cord attaching to the physical person from the Poppet doll, see the cord pulsing with energy, see the energy flowing both ways to and from the doll. Know that this is the connection that will allow for your focused energy and spell to pass through, to reach the physical person. Once this has been done successfully and you have "set" the cord so it is strong and the flow is rhythmic, much like when someone breathes, in nature you can move forward to the next step.

Take a tag and write the person's name on the tag. Take a red string and place the tag on the string, then tie the string around the middle of the doll so that the tag remains in the back. The doll is now ready for the spell you are ready to cast as it has been energized and tagged with a name.

STEP #3 Specific Instruction for your spell
See your particular spell for the next steps. Follow those steps as outline for your specific spell. Following this page is a super easy Doll Pattern you can create. Just copy this page (like a template) add 1/4 inch outline for a seam and make your own poppet

Wolfen Wicca 2
Class #13 Poppet Pattern

By Lady Wolfen Mists © 1990

Poppet Pattern (c) LWM 1992

Don't sew between lines, leave it open for stuffing

Lady Wolfen Mists

Wolfen Wicca 2
Class #13
Poppet of Protection

By Lady Wolfen Mists © 1990

Items needed
- 1 White Voodoo Doll
- 1 Red String
- 1 Rose stick Incense or flower smell
- 1 Name Tag
- 1 Purple String

Cut our Poppet from cloth using template on previous page. Be sure to turn the Poppet inside out so you cant see the stitches and fill with Stuffing. You can get stuffing for pillows at any craft store. Be sure to have collected the items of the "target" person, and place their nail clippings and hair or such, in the open seam after you have stuffed it with stuffing and finish the seam to close the doll. If you are doing this spell for yourself, then use your own hair and nail clippings.

Write the name of the person on the name tag and place it under the doll, you can tie it to the doll with the red string if you want.

This is a variation of a traditional spell that uses a Purple string to protect you and lift you up from negative. It is a simple spell but is quite effective when done properly. This particular spell is usually done on the Full moon around the beginning of Moon Rise

This spell beings with you lighting the above mentioned Incense, and holding the doll, chanting;

"Keep me safe all day through
In all that I will ever do
Stay with me both day and Night
And keep in the path of Light
Do not let me stray away.
Keep me straight both night and day

In your Hands I want lay
As I work throughout the day
Protected from all nasty negative things
Held up on spirited angel like wings

Class #13
Poppet of Protection page 2

Pass the doll through the smoke of the incense and allow the incense to surround the doll, do this 13 times (the number of full moons in a year), in a left to right fashion so as to set the energies that you are casting.

> **"As this smoke surrounds this doll**
> **The same to me so I won't fall**
> **Protective shield envelop me**
> **Keep me safe from all negativity."**

Lay the doll down and pull the purple cord around the doll, visualize your impenetrable protective shield surrounding you. See yourself or the target person in every day life and avoiding situations that may hurt you/them. Then tie 13 knots in the cords as they encircle the doll, one for each full moon. Pass the doll through the Incense once more, and allow the smoke to take your spell out to the universe.

Next place your doll in a special place of honor, like on a shelf. Clean up the left over items and incense. If there is any incense left save it for another day. That's all there is to it, your spell has been cast!

One final note, just "know" that you have cast your spell and it **WILL** be successful! The keys here are belief (as even a little doubt weakens your spell), **Visualization** (you Must "see" these things happening in your minds eye and settle for nothing less). The last key here is knowing that you **want what is best for everyone involved**, not just the individuals involved, but for the entire universe.

Lady Wolfen Mists

Wolfen Wicca 2
Class #13
Get Money Poppet

By Lady Wolfen Mists © 1990

Item Needed;

1 Black Poppet Doll 1 Green String
1 Name Tag 1 stick of Frankincense Incense
2 Red String 1 Set of 3 Pins

Cut our Poppet from cloth using template on previous page. Be sure to turn the Poppet inside out so you can't see the stitches and fill with Stuffing. You can get stuffing for pillows at any craft store. Be sure to have collected the items of the "target" person, and place their nail clippings and hair or such, in the seam in the back of the doll, sew it up as stated on the other page. If you are doing this spell for yourself, then use your own hair and nail clippings. Write the name of the person on the name tag and place it under the doll, you can tie it to the doll with the extra red string if you want.

This is a variation of a traditional spell that uses both the pins included and a red and green cord. It is a simple spell but is quite effective when done properly. This particular spell is usually done on the Full moon around the beginning of Moon Rise.

This spell begins with you holding the doll and chanting;

> "Bring me silver, bring me gold,
> Bring me dollars that will fold.
> I deserve riches, wealth, and money too.
> I send you out my will to do!"

Lay the doll down and pull the red and green cord around the doll, visualize all the money you need coming to you. See yourself a success and without wants or cares. Then tie 3 knots in the cords as they encircle the doll, next take a pin and put 1 pin per knot through each knot to seal in your spell.

Get Money Poppet Page 2

Pass the doll (with pins in place) through the Frankincense Incense and allow the smoke to take your spell out to the universe.

Next place your doll in a place where it will remain undisturbed and hidden from the view of others. Each night for 1 month take the doll out before you go to bed and allow it to sit out, so that it may do your will while you are sleeping (IE. bring wealth to you) then in the morning put it away again where no one will see it.

As good fortune comes your way remove a pin, until all the pins are removed, keep the knots in place. Store the pins in a special place in case you want to use them again. Store the doll in a secret place and keep it safe. If you need to recast the spell, do so, just use fresh cords (green and red) and reuse pins. That's all there is to it, your spell has been cast!

Wolfen Wicca 2
Class #13
Request Knowledge of the Hidden Mysteries
(Seeking Powers and Gifts... Ask Direction)

By Lady Wolfen Mists © 1990

Items Needed

1 White Voodoo Doll	1 Vial Beings of Moon Water Oil	1 Red String
1 Name Tag	1 Purple Candle	1 paper bag

Cut our Poppet from cloth using template on previous page. Be sure to turn the Poppet inside out so you can't see the stitches and fill with Stuffing. You can get stuffing for pillows at any craft store. Be sure to have collected the items of the "target" person (this can be yourself), and place the nail clippings and hair or such, in the seam in the back of the doll, sew it up as stated on the other page.

Now this spell should be done for **7 days** in a row, at approx. the same time every night. Take the purple candle and rub it lightly (every night) with Beings of Light oil. Light the candle and set it in the middle of a table or special burning place. Pick up the doll and hold the doll in both hands and say:

"Great Goddess that created all,
Keep me safe; ne'er let me fall.
Hidden gifts, I ask from thee...
And with wisdom please surroundth me."

(At this point drip purple wax all over the doll, especially the head (crown chakra), approx. 3-9 drops per night wait 13 heartbeats. Then rub the Moon Water oil on the doll, don't saturate it just a drop or two and say the following)

"Hidden Mysteries of the Universe,
In my mind become immersed.
To only be used for Truth and Light,
I seek to become a Guardian with Might."

Continue holding the doll and see the person being given the gifts and wisdom requested. Visualization is the key element here to getting what you ask for. Be sure

Hidden Mysteries Poppet Page 2

to explain in your visualization why you want these gifts, powers or hidden knowledge and how you plan to use it. The Universe will then decide if you are ready to accept the responsibility of such gifts and will give you what you ask for in accordance to what level of enlightenment you are ready for. Remember you can't get to z with out learning all the other letters first. So be clear, concise and open to the universe. Show humility and respect for the order and balance of things and be ready willing and able to accept the responsibility that goes with such a request. Once the visualization stage is complete you can move on to the next step.

Place the doll down in front of the candle; allow candles to burn for a few more minutes. Now say;

> "I send my spell out to the Universe
> With hopes not to make the situation worse.
> In harmony it may abound,
> The Greater Truth will be found.
> Only in the Pure Creators Light I say,
> So Mote It Be, may it be that way."

Then blow out the candles and put away your items (in a drawer works well) so that you can do the spell again for the 7-day period. On the last night just place all the items, not the oil as you can keep it to use again, in a paper bag and place it in the outside trash can. Don't worry about it and don't look at it again, just know that you have cast you spell and it **WILL** be successful!

The keys here are belief (as even a little doubt weakens your spell), **Visualization** (you Must "see" these things happening in your minds eye and settle for nothing less). The last key here is knowing that you **want what is best for everyone involved**, not just the individual who has asked, but for the entire universe. The request for gift to be given, or revealed, must truly come from the heart. The person must be willing to pay the price for those gifts and must be ready to accept. Remember, after all, once given or revealed they can not be returned. It is a loss of innocence and a gaining of advancement in the soul, be sure you are ready!

Lady Wolfen Mists

Wolfen Wicca 2
Class #13
What is a Triskele (Trisklion)

By Lady Wolfen Mists © 1990

The Triskele (Trisklion) is a symbol that has been long used to represent the cycle of life within the world(s) as we know it. The 3 spheres (which include the Land, Sea and Sky) and denote the 3 main aspects of the material world that are found within every object. We see these aspects continually flowing outward and back again to the point of origin.

Triskelion "A Celtic Symbol"
Basically, the Celtic Triskelion symbol refers to the spirit of competition and man's continued progress. The Greek reference to Triskelion correctly means "three-legs," and interestingly enough, this sign does have the appearance of three legs running.

The Celtic Triskelion) symbol(is also called triskele, triquetra or fylfot) There's really a **2-fold meaning**, which encompasses two major parts of symbolism.

First Component:
When observing this symbol, we consider the idea of motion. Each of the branches (angles, legs, protrusions,) are placed in such a way so the symbol appears as if it were in constant forward motion.

What is a Triskele (Trisklion) Page 2

Second Component:

The 3 angles, legs, or branches, that that project, are rather important. Unfortunately, much of the exact meanings are difficult to determine, depending on the location, culture, era, or mythological history. Experts in this area sometimes have a difficult time determining the meanings.

The various representations of the three projections found include:

What Does the Triskelion Symbol Represent?

Action
Competition
Cycles
Moving forward
Progress
Revolution

Meanings of the Three Symbolic Extensions of the Triskelion

Spirit, Mind, Body
Father, Son, Holy Ghost
Mother, Father, Child
Past, Present, Future
Power, Intellect, Love
Creator, Destroyer, Sustainer
Creation, Preservation, Destruction

All of these (and still yet more) can be designated for each of the branches found in the triskelion. It's up to the individual (or originating culture) to offer up these meanings.

So the combination of these two components (motion and triad attributes) lets us conclude that this Celtic symbol tells a story of forward motion in the undertaking to reach understanding of this powerful symbol

It is thought by some that this Celtic symbol may also represent the three Celtic worlds. Which include:

The Otherworld: Where spirits, gods and goddesses live.
The Mortal World: Where humans live along with plants and animals.

Lady Wolfen Mists

What is a Triskele (Trisklion) Page 3

The Celestial World: Where unseen energies live and move about. (IE forces of sun, moon, wind and water.)

Just an interesting side note -the number 3 is often seen as a powerful energy for many infinite reasons. One particular number 3 deals with the 3 phases of the moon (new, half, and full). This is an excellent point because many lunar creatures are portrayed as only having three legs in both Alchemy and early European esoteric artwork.

When we add lunar reasoning to the actual definition of the Triskelion we extend the symbol to mean even more.

Lunar Symbolism and the Triskelion

Feminine
Hidden desire
Illumination
Intuition
Mystery
Spirituality
Subconscious
Subtleness

In reflection, it is easy to see why the Celtic Triskelion symbol definitions are so much more complex than just "3 legged. When you incorporate all the variables of evolution, clarification and motion, you create a far different representation of the Triskelion symbol.

Yet overall, the significance of the Triskelion is different, varied and vast. There are so many opportunities for intense depth and purpose, it is easy to see why the Triskele a such a major part in magick with it energies focusing on the power of 3 all around.

So to summarize, the 3 main accepted Triskelion meanings as follows:

Personal growth
Human personal development
Spiritual expansion

Wolfen Wicca 2
Class #13
Facial Analysis

I thought you might enjoy a brief and quick overview of Face Analysis. Now this is by no means the final word on this subject but it will give you a general overview and let you know if you would like further study in this area. Remember that most followers of Wolfen Wicca are very astute in reading a persons facial movements and body language, so this will give you a place to start from. It is said that Facial analysis is over 90% accurate and many big business firms use it as well as handwriting analysis in their overall interviews.

To Find this Quality/ Trait	Look For this
Administration Skills -	This trait is indicated by the straight or hooked convex nose.
Adventurous -	Those people with high adventurous traits are indicated by protruding cheek bones.
Authoritative -	Indicated by the with of the jaw. A wide jaw line is indicative of an individual who is authoritative, whereas a short jaw line indicates a person who is submissive.
Automatic Resistance -	People whose jaw looks wedge shaped automatically resist under pressure.
Detail Concern -	This trait is indicated by the development of small mounds above each side of the inner eyebrow.
Dry Wit -	Dry wit is indicated by a long upper lip

Lady Wolfen Mists

Entrepreneurial Skills -	This trait is shown by the straightness of the outside rim of the ear.
Exactness -	This is indicated by the vertical furrow between the eyebrows and represents the need for being exact and accurate.
Generosity -	This trait is indicated by the size of the lower lip. The larger the lip, the greater the generosity.
Impulsiveness -	If the lips from the side profile can be clearly viewed, the person is very impulsive
Physical - Needs much activity in life overall	The bony prominence or buldge at the back of the head.
Pride In Appearance -	This is indicated by the shortness of the upper lip. The shorter it is, the stronger the need for a good appearance.
Self Reliance	Indicated by how much the nostril flares out from the nose. People with a large flare are highly self reliant
Serious Mind - people do their job well & take life and work very seriously.	Deep set eyes show serious mindedness.
Sharpness -	This trait is indicated by the sharpness of the facial features as seen from the profile. People who have sharp profile features are very alert.
Skepticism -	Is indicated by a turned down nose
Tenacity -	High tenacity is indicated by a protruding chin, whereas low tenacity is indicated by a receding chin.
Tolerance -	This trait is indicated by the distance between the eyes.

Wolfen Wicca 2
Class #13
Practical: Poppet

By Lady Wolfen Mists © 1990

Create a poppet of your choice here or one of your own creation, How did it go? Do you like the use of poppets?

Notes On Spells or Poppet Work

Notes on Class 13

Lady Wolfen Mists

Wolfen Wicca 2
Our Walk Onward To Initiation
Class #14

© Lady Wolfen Mists Jan.1990
revised 2001

Theory:
    Mirrors of Protection
    Potpourri: Crossing of a loved one
    Invoke Goddess
    Invoke God
    Thou Art Goddess
    Create a Fairy Tree
    Initiation ritual

Practical:
    Do Initiation Ritual

Circle Work:
    What is your inspirational thought for the week.

***Assignment: **Students in your Magickal Journal:**
    Preform the initiation ritual and tell me how it meant. What is your new Magickal Name, remember you are a Lord or Lady now of the 1st degree. This will be reviewed when you submit your work for Initiation ☺

"I Walk On!"

Wolfen Wicca 2
Our Walk Onward To Initiation
Class #14

© Lady Wolfen Mists Jan.1992

Mirrors Of Protection

Please place some mirrors (nothing fancy just plain mirrors) with the attached mark on them (you can paint them on the face of the mirror) reflective side facing away from your home and land entrances, this will not only keep the energies away from you all but it will return the energies to the senders that sent them. The mirrors act as a ward and help to create a sacred sphere, and cant be removed by anything negative. If they are knocked down or such once they are "activated" it wont matter as the essence of the energy has been activated on the astral level and cant be removed except by you who placed it. I often use this to help the land as well as the animals who give so much of their energy on the fight of light and dark.

To activate the mirrors once you have painted the symbols on them say the following

"Lighted path for all to see,
so this mirror connects to thee.
In the place of light and dark balance found at its heart.
Protect and keep all within, and 3 times 10 do we send"

Now just hang the mirrors about where you want protected, the trees, the house, especially the electrical items because the energy there really needs cleansed and purified.

Mirrors Of Protection Page 2

This should create an instant bubble about you all, and allow for a small time of rest and create an invincible wall between you all and that which would cause you pain, harm and negativity. Please remember that taking someone's choices for a bigger agenda is harming others as well and these guys do that second nature so you are just using self defense. This balances all that's going on and the only way it can be broken is by the universal laws (which isn't gonna happen) and removal can only be by the person who placed them up with the deactivation of these tools in a specific manner.

Wolfen Wicca 2
Our Walk Onward To Initiation
Class #14
Crossing of a Loved one Potpourri

(c) Lady Wolfen Mists 1996

This potpourri mix is to be used to call winged Fair Folk and aids in the crossing of a loved one. It aids the person who has died to make an easy and successful crossing by calling the winged ones to aid in the understanding and ease of the crossing. It also aids those left behind in gaining a restful healing sleep and acceptance of the death of someone they loved. The Fae help with the will to move forward in this life.

When mixing this blend be sure to ask the Fae for help. Explain what it is to be used for and how important their help would be. Invite them to add their powers to this magickal mixture and thank them for their compassion and aid.

To use this mixture just set it out in small bowls or bags or simmer pot. If you are using it to aid someone in the release of this life of this life and to aid them in an easy crossing then place in their room in a bag. When you place the bag be sure to explain to them that it's alright for them to move on if the need to and you will be OK. Explain that you will miss them but you will see them again in the Summerland.

If you are using the mixture to aid someone who has already crossed you do essentially the same thing as above but simmer the mixture. As the aroma wafts into the air speak to the one who has crossed over, say all the things you didn't get to say when they were alive, don't worry they will hear you. Cry, if you need to and tell them that you will be alright without them, that their spirit may go and experience it's new adventure. That you will see them again, upon you entrance into the Summerland Give them your blessings and direct them to the Light!

Extra mixture can be stored in a cool dark place, in a glass container and used a needed or given as gifts. Be sure to label and date created.

Items needed:
- 1 cup of Basil Leafs
- 1 cup of Cedar Chips
- 1/4 cup of Comfrey
- 1/4 cup of Elder Chips
- 1/4 cup of Sage
- 1/4 cup of Frankincense Tears
- 1/4 cup of Yarrow

Oils
- 20 drops of Lavender
- 10 drops of Spearmint
- 15 drops of Myrrh
- 10 drops of Frankincense
- 4 drops of Violet

Lady Wolfen Mists

Wolfen Wicca 2
Our Walk Onward To Initiation
Class #14

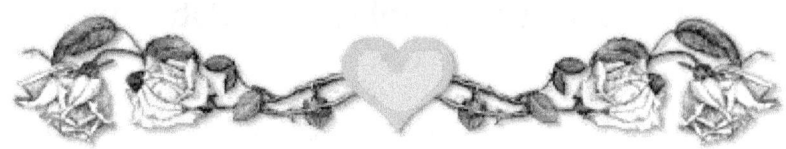

Invocation Of The Goddess

© Lady Wolfen Mists 1997

Most Holy Lady, bathed in silver light,
Keeper of wisdom and knowledge.
Teacher, Healer, Mother, Infinite Creatress, Goddess of All.
We ask your presence here this night.
As we worship, celebrate, share and learn
We look for your guidance, discipline and loving touch.

We, your children, walk the most ancient road,
It sometimes is hard and we beg for a re-freshening of the spirit/soul.
Come to us, abide with us,
Bless and guide us that we may walk in your loving light.
That we may learn the "Hidden" ways.
That we may make you proud and keep your most sacred words etched upon our hearts.

And that this night, as the many yet to come, we call out to you "Mother!"

Wolfen Wicca 2
Our Walk Onward To Initiation
Class #14

Invocation Of The God

© Lady Wolfen Mists 1997

Hear our words that fly on the wind calling out to you
Hear our echo as it rustles on the trees and
Causes the birds to hush and listen.

Come ever near father, especially upon this night
For it is this night that we invite you to unite with us,
We take this time to worship, learn and for merriment.

We know that it is you who keeps us safe in the dark of night,
And you who sees to our sustenance during the long winter.
It is you who lifts us up from those who would prey upon us when we are weak.
You who teaches us Humility, Honor, Love and above all sacrifice

Gracious Father who guides us to the SummerLand, and to the loving arms of the
Mother
We wish to honor you this night

Come Great Stag
Walk with us, Speak to us, Guide us once more

Wolfen Wicca 2
Our Walk Onward To Initiation
Class #14

Thou art Goddess

(C)March 26,1999 at 2:00am, by Lady Wolfen Mists

Once in my confusion, No solace could I find.
I looked to my friends but rebuff was in their minds.
****

I turned once more to logic, if I could understand.
Why was right not always the winner, who leads the hearts of man.
I shouted to the heavens, "Great Goddess, in all your Glory
Are you really real or is my life based on a story?"
****

"Why am I last in most everything, Why am I so poor?
When will the wheel of Karma turn and positive energies find my door?
Steam and Mist rose from my face, as the many tears there poured.
My heart was hurt and broken, my soul was damaged and sore
****

I felt so alone and unwanted, a fool who'd been unveiled
Then I saw the Great White Stag, as through my yard He sailed
He turned at the edge of the yard, and gazed into my eyes
Away faded fears, doubts and the wondering if it was all lies

Wolfen Wicca 2; Our Walk Onward To Initiation

****

And at that very moment, my heart gave out a shout!
For I live within a city, no deer's here to come out
He looked into my soul and my spirit took to flight,
Confusion, doubt, depression, soon hurried out of sight

****

Then away from me He trotted, yet the wind proclaimed forth
"REMEMBER THOU ART GODDESS!"
and have you touched **The Source!**

Wolfen Wicca 2
Our Walk Onward To Initiation
Class #14

How to create a Faery Tree

© Lady Wyntier Song 2014
Used with permission

You can use any small tree 1'-3' tall. You may wish to put it in a large pot if you do not have a back yard or only a small patio area.

You will need:
1 small tree (1-3 feet)
1 quartz crystal (1-3 inches)
1 stick of sandalwood incense
Assorted colored ribbons
1 large flower pot
1 container with water
1 potting Soil to fit flower pot

You will begin by blessing the area you wish to plant the tree (or the pot and soil). To do this you will light the incense and use it to 'draw' a circle 3 times around the pot of soil or the area on the ground you have chosen, while saying the following words of intent:

"Lord and Lady of Light, clear this space.
Remove all negativity from this place.
Bless this water and earth.
Send your energy to grow this tree,
Your own spirit of the earth."

Next you dig the hole in the ground, (or fill the pot 1/3 full with the potting soil. Then place the crystal upright in the bottom of the hole. Next, loosen the roots of the tree, spreading them out slightly, and place gently over the crystal. Now add 4-6 inches of soil, covering the roots completely. Water thoroughly, add the remaining soil. And pat down firmly to remove any air pockets.

Faery Tree Page 2

Say the following:

> "Lord and Lady of Light,
> Send your protection and blessing
> To this little tree spirit,
> A brave guardian of the forest.
> Help it grow tall and strong,
> Spirit of the earth.
> So Mote It Be"

Now you faery tree is ready for the next step. This next part should be done during a full moon.

Take the ribbons you have gathered and draw symbols on them. The symbols should represent your hopes, wishes, blessings, good fortune, or other positive thoughts and affirmations. Now take the ribbons and tie them to different branches on the tree, while concentrating on attracting the friendly Faeries to your home/yard. This magickal tree is supposed to bring good fortune to you and your home.

Wolfen Wicca 2
Our Walk Onward To Initiation
Class #14

Group Initiation Ritual

© 1992 Lady Wolfen Mists

The altar is set as usual, with the circle cast before the members enter. The participants are brought in with their hands bound. They are pushed into the circle one at a time.

Circle caster;
"Who comes to my circle?"

Group response;
"We come in perfect love and trust"

Circle caster; (opens the circle)
"Then welcome in perfect love and perfect trust."

All are gently pushed into the circle by an Initiate that brought them in. All file in and make a half circle in front of the altar. The Initiates now place blind folds upon all members who wish to be come Initiated. After all have been blindfolded the High Priestess calls forth each individual. The person is lead forward and aided to kneel down, they are smudged by the Initiate, with incense.

High Priestess;
"Then blessed be thy hands that they may work in the way of the light. (unbind hands and anoint)

Wolfen Wicca 2; Our Walk Onward To Initiation

Page 2

Blessed be thy heart, that it may always feel compassion, understanding and harmony. (anoint heart)

Blessed be thy mouth, that it may speak with wisdom and tolerance, to aid in the growth of the craft. (anoint mouth)

Blessed be thy ears that they may always hear the ways of the Father and Mother. (anoint ears)

(One of the Initiates gets the newly initiated robes and places it over the Initiate.)

High Priestess:
"Blessed be thy eyed, child, as you once walked in darkness. May you ever see the true beauty in yourself and life. You have begun the enlightened walk, on your chosen path of WICCA. "

(remove blind fold and anoint eyes, hold full length mirror in front of soon to be Initiated)

High Priestess;
"(name), you are now Initiated to the Triple Goddess and her consort, the Lord of Light. Do you practice Solitary or Grove?

Response; "grove"

High Priestess; "What is the name of your Grove?"

Response; (name of grove)

High Priestess;
"Let it be entered in the book of Shadows. On this date,_____,__
Magickal Name, was dedicated into the path of WICCA.
(Kiss Cheek) Blessed Be and welcome!

The Initiate now leads the new Initiate back to their previous spot. The next Member is called and lead forward. When all have been intitate the circle is opened. Gifts are given and words of love are exchanged.

High Priestess:
"This night of celebration continues, from Pre Dedicant to full 1st Degree after a year and a day of study as is tradition. You have come far. never forget those who went before you or the price that they paid. We grow stronger as our numbers grow each year. Let the circle be banished as this rite is at an end. Welcome new 1st Degrees !"

Lady Wolfen Mists

Wolfen Wicca 2
Our Walk Onward To Initiation
Class #14
Solitaire Initiation Ritual

© 1992 Lady Wolfen Mists revised 2002

The altar is set as usual, with the circle cast before the members enter. The New Robe is placed within the circle. Cakes and wine need to be set up. Place a candle that symbolizes you on the altar, leave unlit. After the circle is cast the following is said.

"Great Mother of infinite names. Father who loves and protects me. It is I _say your magickal name here,_ Who comes before you as your child and a seeker of the most ancient ways. As I was in darkness before my pre-dedication I am now in light at the end of my year and a day of study"

Light your unlit candle here, from the Goddess and God flames already burning, allow to burn.

"I come to this most sacred circle to offer my self in service to you in the Way of Wisdom, Love, Light and everlasting positive works. As this holy scent rises so, I pray do my words lift to you. For it is in perfect trust with you and perfect love with you I come before you now and always."

Light Nag Champ or Sandalwood Incense and allow to scent to rise, for at least 13 heartbeats. While this happens think back on your beginnings and how far, you have come. Think on all you have learned and all you have achieved. Realize you are now part of a never ending family with other Wolfen Wicca students and other pagans. A spiritual quest and journey, no longer alone.

Next lift up your new robe and say the following.

"As I put on this robe, I also take the mantle of the Bright Lady and Lord. I become a 1st degree. I pledge my heart and works to my Lady and Lord, and I swear by all I hold sacred and holy to ever do their works, listen to their words and keep my bond and my word. To seal this oath I will now partake of my first cakes and wine as a full Initiate."

Wolfen Wicca 2; Our Walk Onward To Initiation

Page 2

Now do the regular cakes and wine, once done say the following (as it will be stated by Lady Wolfen Mists in the Book of Shadows)

"My Teacher has said I am to announce this to all who have gathered here this night, all Watchers and Guardians. Most esteemed Lady and Lord;
"Let it be entered in the book of Shadows. On this date,_____, Magickal Name, was Initiated into the path of WICCA. I am surely blessed and welcome in Wolfen Wicca as a (*Lady or Lord Magickal name*)! So Mote It Be!

Let the circle be banished as this rite is at an end

Wolfen Wicca 2
Class #14
Practical: Initiation Ritual

By Lady Wolfen Mists © 1990

Do an Initiation ritual and tell me how it went. Now that you are a Lady or Lord can you feel the difference? Do you feel closer to the Goddess and God? Do you feel like you have come Home and the energies surrounding you are lighter. If yes How. if not please explain.

On Becoming Recognized Graduate of this course which results in 1st Degree Level

To; My Students

From : Lady Wolfen Mists

If you are interested in joining this tradition after you finish the classes you can get a hold of me at this e-mail **silverhoofs@att.net** Be sure to mark it *Wolfen Wicca book 2 questions*, I will give you further instructions there.

You will need to send copies of your assignments from your magickal Journal . To the address you will be given through e-mail. You will also need to write a short typed paper. Don't worry about grammar or spelling or anything like that, topic of your choice in Wolfen Wicca

In addition there may be a fee of $50.00 (Fifty dollars) for the Initiation Certificate and for becoming a Lord or Lady of the Wolfen Wicca Tradition. Be sure to include your Magickal Name and how its spelled so we can get it right on your graduation certificate and your mailing address you want the package to come to.

OK that's it, Hope you had a wonderful experience in reading and learning. I am just an e-mail away and will answer your questions as soon as I can. However there may be time delays as there are many of you and my ol' fingers just don't type so good any more (hee hee)

Bright Blessings,

Congratulations on your achievement

Lady Wolfen Mists

For Your Notes

For Your Notes

For Your Notes

Other books by Lady Wolfen Mists & Silver Hoofs

Coming soon or Already Here

* =Coming soon

CHILDREN'S CORNER BOOKS

The Adventures of Knobbly Vol 1 By Addy Venture & A Bud Dee

The adventures of Knobbly the squirrel, his Faery and Forest friends.

Knobbly's life as he ventures from home in the Misty Mountains.

*The Adventures of Knobbly Vol 2 By Addy Venture & A Bud Dee

More Stories about Knobbly

INSPIRATIONAL BOOKS

Stop Kicking My Chair By Lady Wolfen Mists

Working With Angels and the messages given to her over the years, some never before shared

*Tools Of Light By Lady Wolfen Mists

Tools given to her for the world to use from the Angels

WICCA & METAPHYSICAL TOPICS

Wolfen Wicca 101

Basics of Wolfen Wicca to Dedication level-Beginners

Wolfen Wicca 2

Wolfen Wicca 2 to 1st degree level

*Animal Communication Course

(Part 1 of 3 in shape Shifting Series)

Basics and step by step practices to communicating with Animals. Not a beginners course for advanced students

More in the works……

http://www.silverhoofs.com

Lady Wolfen Mists

www.ingramcontent.com/pod-product-compliance
Lightning Source LLC
Chambersburg PA
CBHW080725230426
43665CB00020B/2620